Microwave Cooking ·
Adapting Conventional Recipes

Litton Microwave Cooking Products, Minneapolis, Minnesota

from Litton

CERTIFIED FOR MICROWAVE COOKING

LITTON Microwave Cooking Center

CREDITS:

Design & Production: Cy DeCosse Creative Department, Inc.
Author: Barbara Methven
Home Economists: Jill Crum, Carol Grones
Food Stylist: Muriel Markel
Photographers: Michael Jensen, Ken Greer
Production Coordinators: Bernice Maehren, Nancy McDonough
Consumer Testers: Lee Hartmann, Eileen Hassel, Joan Loonam, Mavis Nagel, Judith Richard, Cathy Troyak
Color Separations: Weston Engraving Co., Inc.
Printing: Moebius Printing Co.

This is no ordinary recipe book. It's like a cooking school in your home, ready to answer questions on the spot. Step-by-step photographs show you how to prepare food for microwaving, what to do during cooking, how to tell when the food is done. A new photo technique shows you how foods look during microwaving.

The foods selected for this book are basic in several ways. All microwave well and demonstrate the advantages of microwaving. They are popular foods you prepare frequently, so the book will be useful in day-to-day cooking. Each food illustrates a principle or technique of microwaving which you can apply to similar recipes you find in magazines or other cookbooks.

This book was designed to obtain good results in all brands of ovens. Techniques may vary from the cookbook developed for your oven. If rotating foods is unnecessary in your oven, that technique may be eliminated. All foods are cooked at either High or 50% power (Medium). The Defrost setting on earlier ovens and Simmer setting on current ovens may be used when Medium is called for. This simplifies the choice of settings while you become familiar with the reasons why different foods require different power levels.

Microwaving is easy as well as fast. The skills you develop with this book will help you make full and confident use of your microwave oven.

The Litton Microwave Cooking Center

Contents

How to Use This Book

This book shows you how to convert your own conventional recipes for microwaving. It's more than just a recipe book, although we hope you'll try the recipes we've adapted and microwave-tested. They illustrate how the directions are used with actual recipes.

Follow these simple steps:

1. Find the chapter which includes the type of food you are preparing and read the conversion guidelines.
2. Identify your recipe by its ingredients and cooking techniques.
3. Follow the specific directions for that food and note any changes you may need to make. The sample recipe shows you how.

Read the Conversion Guidelines

The book is divided into chapters which will be familiar to you from conventional cookbooks, such as, Meats and Main Dishes or Desserts. Each chapter begins with general conversion guidelines. Then, each food category in the chapter has specific directions and an explanation of what was done and why.

Find the Description of Your Recipe

The food categories in each chapter are described by food type, main ingredients and any other ingredients which affect microwaving. We have selected one recipe as an example, but the directions can be applied to any recipe which fits the description. For example, Cooked Chicken in Stirable Sauce is illustrated by Baked Chicken Salad. The same directions apply to Chicken A'la King or Chicken Chow Mein.

Sample Recipe Shows You What to Do

Each food category is illustrated by a tested conventional recipe with simple notations of the changes such as you may want to make yourself on recipe cards or in books. A final microwave recipe is included so you can compare the two versions and prepare the foods which have been tested in all major brands of microwave ovens.

Refer to the Time Box

The yellow boxes with each food category provide a quick reference for an approximate estimate of the time needed. Actual microwaving time for your recipe will depend on several factors. Some of these are: the speed of your oven, voltage in your home or community, the amount of main ingredient in your recipe, the amount of other ingredients, including liquid, and the size and shape of pieces.

One of the most common changes is in recipe yield. Can you double a recipe or cut it in half? General guidelines for changing the size of a recipe are on page 27. If your quantities are different, follow the basic procedures for each specific food, but increase or decrease the time.

How to Use the Index

The index in this book is unique. It lists important ingredients and recipes appearing in the book. It also lists other popular recipes which are not included in the book and refers you to the pages where you will find guidelines for adapting them. As you gain experience in converting recipes, you will learn to identify them by categories. For example, Chicken Cacciatore and Coq Au Vin are Chicken Pieces in Sturdy Sauce and can be converted in the same way as Barbecue Chicken.

What You Need to Know Before You Start

How to Select Recipes for Conversion

While you are learning the techniques of conversion, it's best to start with a familiar recipe. Knowing how the food is supposed to look and taste will help you adapt it for microwaving. If you have not tried the recipe conventionally, make sure the proportions and flavors are pleasing. If you wouldn't like the recipe conventionally, you probably won't care for the microwave version either.

Next, check the list of foods which don't work. These lists are found at the beginning of each chapter. Refer to pages 6 to 8. Is the cooking technique one which can be achieved by microwaving?

Moist cooking is natural to microwaving. Look for conventional recipes which call for liquid, covering or steaming. This indicates that the food needs moisture and should microwave well. If a crisp crust or dry surface is essential to the recipe, it will be more satisfactory when conventionally cooked.

Some foods can be adapted, but will be slightly different when microwaved. Omelets will not brown or crust and cakes will be more tender. You may actually prefer the microwave version.

Stirring or turning foods over helps them microwave evenly. If your conventional recipe allows for stirring or turning, it should adapt easily. A recipe which calls for constant or frequent stirring will be simpler to make by microwave.

If the recipe does not call for stirring, can you include this step in the microwave version? See the recipe for Scalloped Potatoes, page 48. By stirring the casserole, we were able to use High power and take full advantage of microwave speed.

Rotate the dish and reduce the power setting if stirring food would change the recipe too much. The Lasagna on page 56 illustrates this method.

How to Select Power Setting and Time

Look for a similar recipe in this book. Select one with a similar amount and type of liquid, and the same quality and quantity of main bulky ingredients.

High Power **50% Power**

Type of liquid may be sturdy, like chicken broth, which can be microwaved at High power, or delicate, like cream, which may need a lower power setting. Cubed chuck is less tender beef and cannot be microwaved in the same way as higher quality cubed sirloin.

Quantity is important because more food takes more time. If your recipe calls for a different amount of food, you can follow the conversion guidelines, but you will have to adjust the cooking time.

How to Keep It Simple

As you look through this book you will see that many recipes are easy to adapt. Others need only minor changes, which will become familiar as you gain experience. A few are more difficult because they require understanding of what happens to foods during microwaving.

Recipes which require extensive changes in ingredients and repeated trial and error testing have not been included in this book. If a food must be reformulated for microwaving, we feel you would be happier with the results if you follow a microwave-tested recipe.

Easy to adapt recipes use the same ingredients. The only changes needed for this dip are a microwave oven-safe utensil and a shorter cooking time.

Moderate changes may be recommended in piece size and

the amount of liquid and seasonings. Small, uniform pieces not only cook faster, they microwave more evenly.

When the guidelines suggest reducing the liquid, start with the minimum amount and add more during cooking if it is needed to make the microwave version match conventional results.

Use less salt and season to taste after cooking. Small amounts of herbs and spices usually require no change.

More difficult recipes, like Hollandaise Sauce, may use the same ingredients but require a microwaving technique which is very different from the conventional method.

How to Substitute a Different Ingredient

Most substitutions you make conventionally will work in microwaving, too. If you prefer parsley flakes or instant onion instead of the fresh product, use them in microwaving, following the directions on the packages. Most seasonings are interchangeable. If the recipe calls for an herb you don't care for, substitute one you like.

Some substitutions are recommended for microwaving. Process cheeses melt more smoothly and are easier to use than dry or hard natural cheeses.

Substitute quick-cooking rice for converted or raw rice. It will be tender in the short time it takes to microwave the other ingredients in a casserole.

Be more cautious with substitutions which will affect the power setting or microwaving time or method.

Cream substituted for milk may need a lower power of 50% (Medium) and double the time. If you substitute converted for quick-cooking rice, you must microwave the rice until it is partially tender before adding other ingredients. When you exchange flour for cornstarch in a sauce, you should increase the amount as you would conventionally and stir the sauce more often.

Some substitutions affect the consistency of a dish. If you wish to reduce calories, you may use yogurt in place of sour cream, but should reduce the amount because it is more liquid.

How to Select the Microwave Method for a Conventional Recipe

Most of the cooking methods called for in conventional recipes can be achieved by microwaving, too. This section lists common conventional cooking terms with a description of the method, followed by directions for producing a similar result when microwaving.

Two conventional cooking methods can't be adapted to microwaving. Don't attempt to deep-fat fry; it can be dangerous. Oven broiling cannot be achieved with microwaves, although you can melt cheese toppings or heat sandwiches when a brown and crusty surface is not essential to the recipe.

Compare Conventional and Microwave Cooking Methods

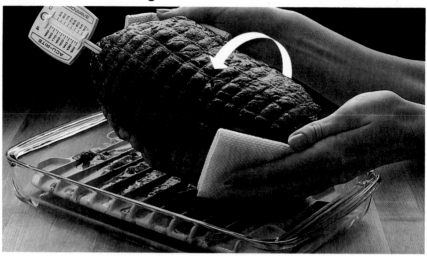

Roast. Meat is elevated on a rack set in a shallow pan and cooked uncovered to desired internal temperature. Baste occasionally to keep surface moist.

Microwave Roast. Place meat on microwave rack in baking dish. Do not cover. Microwave at 50% (Medium) or 30% (Medium-low) to desired internal temperature, using a microwave thermometer or probe. Basting is unnecessary, but meat should be turned over after half the cooking time.

Braise, Stew, Casserole-Roast. Meat, fruit, or vegetables, sometimes browned first, are simmered with flavoring liquid in a covered pan, using range top or oven. More liquid is added to a stew than a braise. Casserole-roasted meats are cooked on a bed of moist vegetables without additional liquid.

Microwave Braise, Stew, Casserole-Roast. Omit browning. Reduce amount of liquid in braises and stews. Cover tightly or use a cooking bag. Microwave meats at 50% (Medium) or 30% (Medium-low).

6

Poach. Fish, chicken, eggs or fruit are immersed in liquid held at a feeble simmer in an open pan.

Microwave Poach. Reduce liquid to 1 cup or less to produce steam and carry flavorings. Cover dish tightly with plastic wrap. Power setting depends on the type of food.

Steam. Food is elevated on a rack set over boiling water, or container of food is surrounded with simmering water in a covered pot. In either case, water does not touch food.

Microwave Steam. Moist foods may be microwaved in tightly covered dish without water. Place mold of delicate food, like mousse, in dish of hot water and microwave uncovered.

Sauté. Food is seared or lightly browned in butter or oil, then covered and simmered over low heat. Moist vegetables or small amount of liquid are added to meat or chicken.

Microwave Sauté. Omit browning and fat, unless desired for flavor. Microwave, covered, at power setting suitable for food.

Pan-fry, Pan-broil. Food is cooked uncovered to retain the crisp, dry surface. Add a small amount of butter or oil for pan-frying. No fat is used for pan-broiling.

Microwave Pan-fry, Pan-broil. Preheat browning utensil as manufacturer directs. Add fat if pan-frying none if broiling. Microwave food on both sides, uncovered.

Stir-fry. Small pieces of food are fried quickly in a small amount of oil and stirred constantly to prevent sticking. Quick-cooking foods are added last. Pan may be de-glazed with liquid to form a sauce.

Microwave Stir-Fry. Preheat 10-in. browning dish as directed. Add oil and long-cooking foods. (Add quick-cooking foods later.) Stir every 2 minutes. Make sauce, if desired.

Bake. Food is placed in pre-heated oven and cooked, covered or uncovered, at the recommended temperature. Since air is dry, a pan of water may be placed in oven when steam is required.

Microwave Bake. Microwave food, covered or uncovered, at recommended power setting. Oven is never preheated and air is not hot or dry.

Estimating Microwave Time & Testing for Doneness

The major difference between a conventional recipe and the microwave adaptation is in cooking time. The sample recipes in this book were tested in ovens of 600 to 650 watts. Some microwave ovens have a higher wattage. If your oven is one of these, check your food for doneness before the minimum time.

Microwave ovens differ in speed and evenness of cooking. Some operate most efficiently with a medium food load and may be slower with light or heavy loads.

The cookbook which came with your oven can help you estimate whether the food will be done in the minimum or maximum times suggested here. If the book recommends more frequent stirring or turning of food, the extra attention may be needed to give good results with your oven's cooking pattern.

In general, the microwaving time will be approximately ¼ to ½ of the conventional time, unless the food is one which needs more time to rehydrate or tenderize. Many people believe that times are critical in microwaving and that a few seconds difference can ruin the food. This is not true. In microwaving, as in conventional cooking, times help you estimate how long the food may take, but you are the final judge of when it is done.

A microwave scale is a useful tool for recipe conversion. It estimates cooking time according to weight of food and power setting.

Watch. Check the progress of cooking frequently. This is easy to do with a microwave oven; you can interrupt cooking without harm to the food.

Add a little more liquid if you see it is needed to match the consistency of your conventional recipe.

Stir, turn or rotate the food if it appears to be cooking unevenly.

Test. For most recipes, the microwave tests for doneness are the same as conventional. It's a good idea to check for doneness at the minimum time. You can always cook longer, but overcooking can be a serious problem. Be sure to allow standing time when the food requires it.

Taste. The first time you convert a recipe, reduce the salt, and correct to taste when cooking is completed. Tasting will also help you judge tenderness, texture and consistency.

Sample Recipe Shows How We Did It

In this book you'll find typical conventional recipes with notes on the changes needed to convert them for microwaving, plus a fully tested microwave version of each recipe. Use them as a guide to converting similar recipes from your own collection.

Some recipes need little change except timing. Small changes in ingredients, utensil or cooking techniques are noted on the sample recipes. Where it would be helpful, we've included an explanation of the changes in the conversion guidelines for each food category.

Why This Recipe Was Selected

In this conventional saute, the chicken is covered after searing. This means that a browned flavor and crisp surface are not part of the recipe, since both are lost in conventional cooking when a pan is covered. The chicken should have the same flavor and texture when microwaved.

What Was Changed and Why

Conventionally, the chicken is seared in butter to prevent sticking, and oil is added to keep the chicken from blackening. In microwave cooking, searing is not necessary, so that step was omitted. The paprika in this recipe will give the chicken an attractive color without browning. If you are concerned about cholesterol, skin the chicken before cooking.

In the microwave version, butter was not needed to prevent sticking, but some butter was used for flavor and to help the paprika adhere to the meat. The oil was omitted because the butter will not burn. Since paprika is a mild seasoning, we used the same amount, but cut down the salt and pepper. Some wine was added for flavor; we reduced the quantity because liquid will not evaporate during microwaving. You may use the full amount for more wine flavor, but sauce will be slightly thinner.

Cooking time was based on another microwave recipe. To heat the cream, we reduced the power to 50% (Medium). This is especially important when sour cream is used, because it breaks down at high temperatures. To estimate heating time for your oven, check the manufacturer's cookbook for the time needed to heat 1 cup of a milk-based soup or beverage.

What We Learned

In the microwave version, we found it necessary to skim the cooking juices before finishing the sauce. Microwaving clarifies butter and extracts more fat from the chicken.

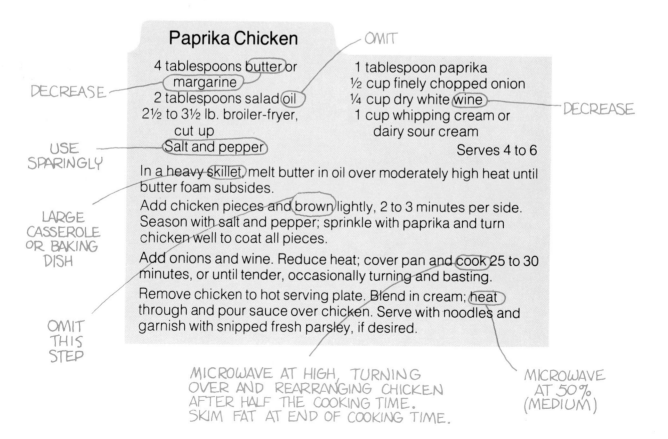

Paprika Chicken

OMIT

DECREASE

4 tablespoons butter or margarine
2 tablespoons salad oil
2½ to 3½ lb. broiler-fryer, cut up
Salt and pepper

1 tablespoon paprika
½ cup finely chopped onion
¼ cup dry white wine
1 cup whipping cream or dairy sour cream

DECREASE

Serves 4 to 6

USE SPARINGLY

LARGE CASSEROLE OR BAKING DISH

In a heavy skillet, melt butter in oil over moderately high heat until butter foam subsides.

Add chicken pieces and brown lightly, 2 to 3 minutes per side. Season with salt and pepper; sprinkle with paprika and turn chicken well to coat all pieces.

Add onions and wine. Reduce heat; cover pan and cook 25 to 30 minutes, or until tender, occasionally turning and basting.

OMIT THIS STEP

Remove chicken to hot serving plate. Blend in cream; heat through and pour sauce over chicken. Serve with noodles and garnish with snipped fresh parsley, if desired.

MICROWAVE AT HIGH, TURNING OVER AND REARRANGING CHICKEN AFTER HALF THE COOKING TIME. SKIM FAT AT END OF COOKING TIME.

MICROWAVE AT 50% (MEDIUM)

Converted Chicken Recipe

2½ to 3½ lb. broiler-fryer, cut up
2 tablespoons butter or margarine
Salt and pepper
1 tablespoon paprika
½ cup finely chopped onion
2 tablespoons dry white wine
1 cup whipping cream or dairy sour cream

Serves 4 to 6

Skin chicken, if desired. In large casserole or baking dish, melt butter at High ¾ to 1 minute. Add chicken; turn to coat lightly. Season lightly with salt and pepper. Sprinkle half the paprika over chicken. Turn pieces over; arrange meatiest portions to outside of dish. Sprinkle with paprika.

Add onion and wine; cover tightly. Microwave at High 15 to 18 minutes, or until juices run clear, turning over and rearranging after half the time.

Remove chicken to serving plate, cover with foil. Skim fat from juices. Blend in cream. Reduce power to 50% (Medium). Microwave uncovered, 1½ to 2½ minutes, or until heated through. Pour sauce over chicken, garnish with snipped parsley, if desired, serve with noodles.

14 to 20 minutes

2½ to 3 lb. broiler-fryer

Key Steps in Converting the Paprika Chicken Recipe

Times for cooking the chicken and heating the sauce were estimated from another microwave cookbook.

Paprika in the recipe serves as a browning agent as well as adding a light seasoning.

Remove fat from juices before finishing sauce. Microwaving extracts more fat from meat.

Appetizers

Adapting Appetizers

Appetizers are a good place to start learning to adapt recipes. Those which are simply heated need no change except a microwave utensil and time. Others require only small changes in ingredients. See sample recipes for methods and approximate times.

This section features hot appetizers because microwaving makes these specialties easy to serve, but remember to use your oven when preparing cold appetizers, too. Use it to soften cream cheese or steam chicken quickly for salads and spreads.

Microwaving reheats foods without drying them out, so many dishes can be prepared in advance. Some appetizers are better when microwaved, while others have the same quality in far less time.

Microwave utensils can be used for both cooking and serving. Use a paper plate or napkin under crackers and breads to absorb moisture from steam trapped between food and plate.

No change except heating time is needed for most dips, spreads and canapes.

Microwave Tips for Appetizers

Improvise almost-instant canapes with a cracker, a pinch of grated cheese and a garnish such as sliced olives, onions, sausage or anchovy filets.

Stuffed mushrooms hold their shape when microwaved. Conventionally, they soften and are difficult to serve as finger food.

Substitute an ordinary casserole for elaborate warming equipment, such as a chafing dish, fondue pot or hot plate. Return dish to the oven and reheat as often as needed.

Reduce amount of sauce when cooking or heating meats; it will not evaporate in the short microwaving time.

Reheat conventionally baked cream puffs and turnovers on a napkin just before serving.

Some Things That Don't Work and Why

Puff Pastries, both fresh and frozen, need dry heat to crisp. Pastries puff in the microwave oven, but fall when removed.

Turnovers, like double crust pies, do not bake on the bottom.

Broiled Canape Toppings become bubbly but will not be crusty and browned.

Fried Appetizers can be made in a browning dish, but not in an ordinary casserole. A browning dish keeps frozen egg rolls crisp.

Biscuits Wrapped Around Sausages do not brown and become soggy because they absorb moisture from the meat.

Pastry-Wrapped Olives must be specially formulated for microwaving because they require a very dry mixture.

15

Hot Dips: Cream Cheese Base

Dips which are heated, not cooked, need no change in ingredients. Cream cheese can be softened at High power, but needs stirring toward the end of cooking time. Reduce power to 50% (Medium) to heat dip evenly without excessive stirring. Total time depends on the amount and starting temperature of ingredients. Dip may be mixed in advance and refrigerated, but will take about twice as long to heat.

Hot Crab Dip

1 package (8-oz.) cream cheese
3 tablespoons mayonnaise
1 tablespoon Worcestershire sauce

2 teaspoons lemon juice
1 green onion, chopped
1 can (6½-oz.) crab meat

Makes 1½ cups

OMIT.

Preheat oven to 350°. *1 QT. SERVING DISH*

MICROWAVE AT HIGH STIRRING AFTER 30 SECONDS, THEN EVERY 15 SECONDS.

In small oven-proof dish, soften cream cheese with a fork. Blend in mayonnaise, Worcestershire sauce, lemon juice and onion. Set aside.

MICROWAVE AT 50% (MEDIUM) UNTIL HOT STIRRING AFTER 2 MINUTES, THEN EVERY MINUTE.

Rinse crab in cool water; drain. Flake meat and remove cartilage. Stir into cream cheese mixture. Bake 15 to 20 mintues, or until hot.

Converted Hot Crab Dip

1 pkg. (8-oz.) cream cheese
3 tablespoons mayonnaise
1 tablespoon Worcestershire sauce
2 teaspoons lemon juice
1 green onion, chopped
1 can (6½-oz.) crab meat

Makes 1½ cups

In 1-qt. serving dish, soften cream cheese at High 45 to 60 seconds, stirring after 30 seconds, then every 15 seconds. Blend in mayonnaise, Worcestershire sauce, lemon juice and onion. Set aside.

Rinse crab in cool water; drain. Flake meat and remove cartilage. Stir into cream cheese mixture. Microwave at 50% (Medium) 4 to 6 minutes, or until mixture is hot, stirring after 2 minutes, then every minute.

3 to 8½ minutes

1½ cups

Hot Dips: Process or Natural Cheese Base

Microwave speed is an asset when melting cheese, but care must be taken not to overheat cheese or it will become stringy and tough. Process and soft to medium natural cheeses, such as Mozzarella, Monterey Jack and some Cheddars melt readily at 50% (Medium) with a minimum of stirring. Diced or cubed Swiss and hard Cheddar are more difficult to melt. Grate them, or substitute a softer cheese. In this conventional recipe, simmering the tomatoes reduces liquid and concentrates flavor. To achieve this result by microwaving, we used High power. It required less time and stirring than conventionally.

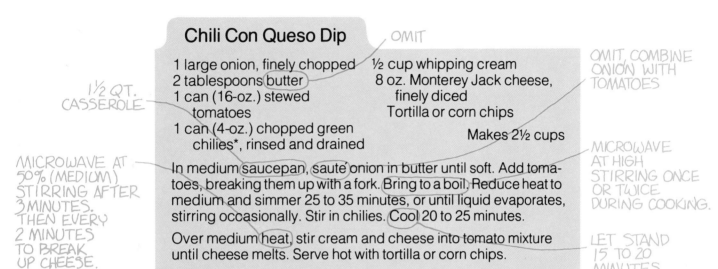

Chili Con Queso Dip

OMIT

1½ QT. CASSEROLE

MICROWAVE AT 50% (MEDIUM) STIRRING AFTER 3 MINUTES. THEN EVERY 2 MINUTES TO BREAK UP CHEESE.

OMIT, COMBINE ONION WITH TOMATOES

MICROWAVE AT HIGH STIRRING ONCE OR TWICE DURING COOKING.

LET STAND 15 TO 20 MINUTES.

1 large onion, finely chopped
2 tablespoons butter
1 can (16-oz.) stewed
    tomatoes
1 can (4-oz.) chopped green
    chilies*, rinsed and drained

½ cup whipping cream
8 oz. Monterey Jack cheese,
    finely diced
Tortilla or corn chips

Makes 2½ cups

In medium saucepan, saute onion in butter until soft. Add tomatoes, breaking them up with a fork. Bring to a boil. Reduce heat to medium and simmer 25 to 35 minutes, or until liquid evaporates, stirring occasionally. Stir in chilies. Cool 20 to 25 minutes.

Over medium heat, stir cream and cheese into tomato mixture until cheese melts. Serve hot with tortilla or corn chips.

*For "hot" peppers, start with ½ can; add to taste before serving.

Converted Chili Con Queso Dip

1 large onion, finely chopped
1 can (16-oz.) stewed tomatoes
1 can (4-oz.) chopped green
    chilies, rinsed and drained
½ cup whipping cream
8 oz. Monterey Jack cheese,
    finely diced
Tortilla or corn chips

Makes 2½ cups

In a 1½-qt. casserole, combine onion and tomatoes. Break up tomatoes with a fork. Microwave at High 20 to 25 minutes, or until moisture evaporates, stirring once or twice. Stir in chilies. Let stand 15 to 20 minutes.

Stir in cream and cheese. Microwave at 50% (Medium) 5 to 8½ minutes, or until cheese melts and dip is hot, stirring after 3 minutes, then every 2 minutes. Serve hot with chips.

3½ to 8½ minutes

2 cups. Time is for melting 8-oz. cheese only

Canapes

Mixtures for heated canapes need no change in ingredients. The canape base should be a very crisp, dry cracker which will complement the flavor of the topping. Fried toast fingers are unsuitable because they become soggy during microwaving. Assemble canapes just before heating. If they are prepared in advance, moisture in the topping will soften the cracker. If you do not wish to serve canapes on paper plates, remove them to a serving dish or line the serving plate with paper napkins. Paper absorbs steam which can collect between cracker and plate. Add garnishes, such as snipped parsley, sliced olives or salted almonds after microwaving.

Chicken Ham Canape

1 can (5-oz.) chunk chicken, finely chopped
1 can (4½-oz.) deviled ham
1 package (4-oz.) shredded Cheddar cheese
¼ cup chopped green onion
36 round buttery crackers

Makes 36

OMIT

Preheat oven to 400°.

Combine chicken, ham, cheese and onion.

Arrange crackers on baking sheet. Place 1 tablespoon spread on each cracker.

Bake 4 to 6 minutes or until cheese melts and spread is hot.

ARRANGE 12 ON UNCOATED PAPER PLATE.   MICROWAVE AT HIGH ROTATING PLATE ¼ TURN AFTER 20 SECONDS.

Pizza on a Cracker

36 melba toast rounds or dry crisp crackers
1 can (6-oz.) tomato paste
3 oz. pepperoni, thinly sliced
¾ cup shredded mozzarella cheese
1 teaspoon basil

Makes 36

OMIT

Preheat oven to 400°.

Place crackers on large, ungreased, baking sheet.

Spread ½ teaspoon tomato paste on each cracker. Top each with 1 slice pepperoni, 1 teaspoon shredded cheese; sprinkle with basil.

Bake 3 to 5 minutes, or until cheese is melted.

ARRANGE 12 ON UNCOATED PAPER PLATE.   MICROWAVE AT HIGH ROTATING PLATE ¼ TURN AFTER 20 SECONDS.

Converted Chicken Ham Canape

1 can (5-oz.) chunk chicken, finely chopped
1 can (4½-oz.) deviled ham
1 package (4-oz.) shredded Cheddar cheese
¼ cup chopped green onion
36 round buttery crackers

Makes 36

Combine chicken, ham, cheese and onion.

Arrange 12 crackers on paper plate. Place 1 tablespoon spread on each cracker.

Microwave at High 30 to 60 seconds, or until cheese melts and spread is hot, rotating plate ¼ turn after 20 seconds. Repeat with remaining ingredients.

20 to 60 seconds

12 crackers per plate with topping.

Converted Pizza on a Cracker

36 melba toast rounds or dry crisp crackers
1 can (6-oz.) tomato paste
3 oz. pepperoni, thinly sliced
¾ cup shredded mozzarella cheese
1 teaspoon basil

Makes 36

Place 12 crackers on uncoated paper plate.

Spread ½ teaspoon tomato paste on each cracker. Top each with 1 slice pepperoni, 1 teaspoon shredded cheese; sprinkle with basil.

Microwave at High 30 to 60 seconds, or until cheese is melted, rotating plate ¼ turn after 20 seconds. Repeat with remaining ingredients.

20 to 60 seconds

12 crackers per plate with topping.

Stuffed Mushrooms

Microwaved stuffed mushrooms are better than conventionally baked because they retain their flavor and shape and are easier for guests to handle. Delicate fillings, like cream cheese, will not break down during heating. Stuffed mushrooms are low in calories and carbohydrates and can be served as an appetizer or side dish on anybody's diet. The only change needed to convert a mushroom stuffing is to reduce the amount of butter used. Buttery fillings separate.

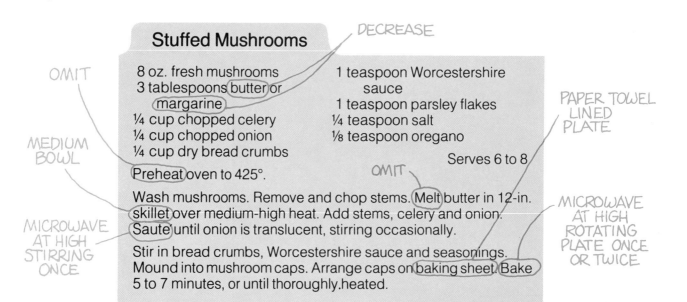

Stuffed Mushrooms

DECREASE

OMIT

8 oz. fresh mushrooms
3 tablespoons butter or margarine
¼ cup chopped celery
¼ cup chopped onion
¼ cup dry bread crumbs

1 teaspoon Worcestershire sauce
1 teaspoon parsley flakes
¼ teaspoon salt
⅛ teaspoon oregano

Serves 6 to 8

PAPER TOWEL LINED PLATE

MEDIUM BOWL

Preheat oven to 425°.

OMIT

Wash mushrooms. Remove and chop stems. Melt butter in 12-in. skillet over medium-high heat. Add stems, celery and onion. Saute until onion is translucent, stirring occasionally.

MICROWAVE AT HIGH STIRRING ONCE

Stir in bread crumbs, Worcestershire sauce and seasonings. Mound into mushroom caps. Arrange caps on baking sheet. Bake 5 to 7 minutes, or until thoroughly heated.

MICROWAVE AT HIGH ROTATING PLATE ONCE OR TWICE

Converted Stuffed Mushrooms

8 oz. fresh mushrooms
2 tablespoons butter or margarine
¼ cup chopped celery
¼ cup chopped onion
¼ cup dry bread crumbs
1 teaspoon Worcestershire sauce
1 teaspoon parsley flakes
¼ teaspoon salt
⅛ teaspoon oregano

Serves 6 to 8

Wash mushrooms. Remove and chop stems. Combine stems, butter and vegetables in bowl. Microwave at High 1½ to 2½ minutes, or until vegetables are tender-crisp, stirring once.

Stir in remaining ingredients. Mound into mushroom caps. Arrange caps on paper towel-lined plate, larger caps to outside of plate. Microwave 1½ to 3 minutes, or until thoroughly heated, rotating plate once or twice.

1½ to 4½ minutes
8-oz. stuffed mushrooms

20

Cheese Sticks

Recipes for cheese pastry vary in the proportion of butter to flour, but are similar to pie crust. If your recipe calls for liquid, use just enough to make the particles adhere.

This conventional recipe calls for an ungreased cookie sheet, but we found that the microwaved cheese sticks were difficult to remove unless the baking surface was lined with wax paper. Cheese sticks may bake unevenly if baking sheet is placed directly on oven floor. Elevating on a rack or inverted saucer moves the sticks into a different pattern of microwave energy.

Cheese Sticks

6 tablespoons butter or margarine
¾ cup grated Cheddar cheese

¾ cup flour
¼ teaspoon salt
2 to 3 drops hot pepper sauce

Makes 2½ to 3½ dozen

OMIT — Preheat oven to 375°.

Using electric mixer, cream butter and cheese. Mix in flour, salt and hot pepper sauce until mxiture resembles soft cookie dough.

Turn mixture out on floured board. Sprinkle with flour. Roll out to ⅛-in. thickness, flouring lightly as needed. Cut into strips ½-in. wide and 2½ to 3-in.long. Place on ungreased cookie sheet. Bake 10 to 15 minutes, or until firm.

PLACE STICKS ON CARDBOARD OR MICROWAVE BAKING SHEET LINED WITH WAX PAPER ELEVATE ON RACK OR INVERTED SAUCER

MICROWAVE AT HIGH.

Converted Cheese Sticks

6 tablespoons butter or margarine
¾ cup grated Cheddar cheese
¾ cup flour
¼ teaspoon salt
2 to 3 drops hot pepper sauce

Makes 2½ to 3½ dozen

Cream butter and cheese with electric mixer. Mix in flour, salt and pepper sauce until mixture resembles soft cookie dough.

Turn mixture out on floured board. Sprinkle with flour. Roll out to ⅛-in. thickness, flouring lightly as needed. Cut into strips ½-in. wide and 2½ to 3-in. long.

Line a microwave baking sheet or 12×12-in. sheet of cardboard with wax paper. Place cheese sticks on paper. Elevate baking sheet on roasting rack or inverted saucer. Microwave at High 3½ to 5½ minutes, or until firm.

3 to 7 minutes
2½ to 3 dozen

21

Meat Tidbits

Chicken wings, cocktail wieners, spare ribs or cubed ham make popular appetizers. To convert them to microwaving, follow the suggestions given here and consult a microwave cookbook for the cooking method and time recommended for your main ingredients. Guidelines for converting appetizer meatballs are on page 41.

If your recipe calls for gravy, barbecue or sweet-sour sauce, reduce the amount by ¼ to ½. All you need is just enough sauce to cover the meat. In this sample recipe, no change was required.

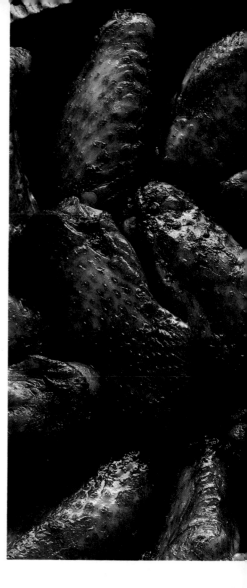

Marinated Chicken Wings

2 lbs. chicken wings
½ cup soy sauce
½ teaspoon ginger
⅛ teaspoon garlic powder

Serves 8 to 10

Cut off and discard wing tips. Separate remainder of each wing into two portions.

Combine soy sauce, ginger and garlic powder in 12×8-in. baking pan or a 1½-qt. casserole. Add wing portions and stir to coat.

Marinate wings at room temperature several hours or in the refrigerator overnight, turning several times.

Preheat oven to 350°. Bake uncovered for 50 to 60 minutes, or until chicken is fork tender, stirring after half the cooking time.

DISH *OMIT* *MICROWAVE AT HIGH*

Bacon Tidbits

Bacon appetizers are a good choice for microwaving. Bacon-wrapped tidbits also convert easily. If the filling is cooked or canned (olives, water chestnuts, oysters, etc.), partially cook the bacon by microwaving about half the time before wrapping it around the filling. This can be done in advance. The bacon will finish cooking in the time it takes to heat the center. Use uncooked bacon to wrap raw fillings, such as chicken livers and microwave until bacon is cooked.

BACON MICROWAVES WELL

Deviled Bacon

1 egg
½ teaspoon dry mustard
¼ teaspoon cayenne pepper
1 teaspoon cider vinegar
1 teaspoon soy sauce
6 slices bacon
½ cup seasoned bread
    crumbs

Makes 2 to 3 dozen

Preheat oven to 350°.

In small bowl, blend together egg, mustard, cayenne, vinegar and soy sauce. Dip each piece of bacon in egg mixture. Dredge in bread crumbs. Place on rack in baking pan. Bake 20 minutes, or until crisped. Cut into serving size pieces.

OMIT *USE PAPER TOWELS.* *MICROWAVE AT HIGH, LET STAND.*

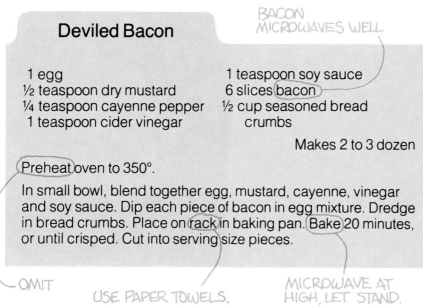

Converted Marinated Chicken Wings

2 lbs. chicken wings
½ cup soy sauce
½ teaspoon ginger
⅛ teaspoon garlic powder

Serves 8 to 10

Cut off and discard wing tips. Separate remainder of each wing into two portions.

Combine soy sauce, ginger and garlic powder in 12×8-in. baking dish. Add wings and stir to coat.

Marinate at room temperature several hours or refrigerate overnight, turning several times.

Discard all but ¼ cup marinade. Cover dish with wax paper. Microwave at High 7½ to 10½ minutes, or until fork tender, stirring after half the cooking time so least cooked portions are brought to outside of the dish.

NOTE: If wings were refrigerated, increase time by 2 to 4½ minutes.

6 to 12 minutes.

2 lbs. chicken and ½ to 1 cup sauce. Temperature of chicken will affect time.

Converted Deviled Bacon

1 egg
½ teaspoon dry mustard
¼ teaspoon cayenne pepper
1 teaspoon cider vinegar
1 teaspoon soy sauce
6 slices bacon
½ cup seasoned bread crumbs

Makes 2 to 3 dozen

In small bowl, blend together egg, mustard, cayenne, vinegar and soy sauce. Dip each piece of bacon in egg mixture. Dredge in bread crumbs. Place on several layers of paper towel. Cover with paper towel. Microwave at High 4½ to 6 minutes, or until crisp. Let stand 2 to 3 minutes. Cut into serving size pieces.

4 to 7 minutes

6 slices of bacon.

Meats & Main Dishes

Converting Meats and Main Dishes

Most meats and main dishes are easy to adapt for microwaving. Look for conventional recipes which call for steaming, covering or stirring. Small pieces and moist or saucy foods microwave well in a fraction of the conventional time.

Fat. Many conventional recipes call for fat to keep meat from sticking to the pan during browning. Since browning is omitted and sticking is not a problem in microwaving, you can usually eliminate fat or use a minimum amount simply for flavor.

Liquid. Generally, you should reduce the amount of liquid, especially in recipes which call for a great deal of moisture or long baking times. When converting a recipe for the first time, reduce the liquid by about ⅓ and add more if necessary to achieve a consistency similar to the conventional dish.

Remember that dry foods, such as uncooked rice or pasta, absorb moisture as they tenderize. The will require a similar amount of liquid when microwaved.

High Altitudes. If you live in a high altitude, you are accustomed to making changes in liquid. Microwave recipes need less adjusting than conventional ones because of the shorter cooking time and minimal evap-

oration. When you are converting a familiar recipe which works conventionally at your altitude, follow the guidelines given in this book. A longer microwaving time will probably be needed. If you have not tried the recipe before, estimate the changes you would make conventionally and then reduce the moisture slightly.

Seasonings. Use slightly less seasoning and correct to taste after microwaving. In this book, we reduced the amount of salt if it was over 1 teaspoon, but made no change in small quantities of herbs or spices.

Power Levels. Select a power level which is appropriate for the

Select recipes which call for cooking techniques used in microwaving. Naturally moist foods and saucy main dishes are easiest to convert.

Reduce liquid by ⅓. Reserve remaining liquid and add if needed during cooking.

Omit or reduce fats. A small amount may be used for flavor, if desired.

Sturdy High
Sauces = Power

Delicate Medium
Sauces = Power

Use High power for foods cooked in sturdy sauces made with tomatoes, broth or wine. Reduce power to 50% (Medium) for delicate sauces containing cream, sour cream or cheese, especially if they cannot be stirred during microwaving.

type of food. Tender meats can be microwaved at High unless they are cooked in a delicate sauce containing eggs or cream. Less tender meats should be tightly covered and microwaved at 50% (Medium).

Timing. For most dishes, microwaving time will be about ¼ to ⅓ the conventional cooking time. Less time will be saved with foods which require a lower power level to tenderize or time to rehydrate or develop flavor.

Microwave long-cooking ingredients until almost tender before adding quick-cooking or delicate foods. To save time and simplify microwaving, substitute quick-cooking rice, pre-cooked dried beans or pasta for the long-cooking form.

Casserole Toppings.
Microwaved casseroles will not crust or brown on top, but can be given a dry, crisp surface when a topping is added after the last stirring. If your recipe calls for a topping of dry bread crumbs, substitute crushed croutons which absorb less moisture and stay crisp. Other excellent toppings are crushed potato or corn chips, crushed canned onion rings, or a mixture of grated cheese and crumbs.

Changing Yield. If you are increasing or decreasing recipe yield, make sure you have the right size dish. Depth of food should be the same as the original recipe. If the dish is too small, food may boil over; if the dish is too large the layer of food will be thinner, which will affect the speed and evenness of cooking. Generally half a recipe will take ⅓ less microwaving time. A double recipe will take about ½ to ⅔ more time. If you are doubling a recipe, decrease the liquid by ¼ to ⅓. These changes in time and liquid apply to recipes already converted for microwaving.

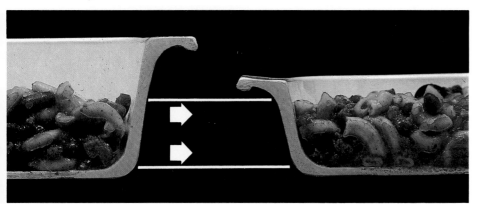

Select a casserole which will maintain food depth when increasing or decreasing yield. Allow enough space to prevent boil-over.

Add quick-cooking or delicate ingredients toward the end of microwaving time.

Sprinkle on toppings after the final stirring to give casseroles a crisp, colorful surface.

Some Things That Don't Work and Why

Deep-fried foods should not be microwaved because fat reaches dangerously high temperatures.

Fried Pork Chops are not satisfactory, even in a browning dish. Chops need moisture to tenderize.

Double Crust pot pies will not bake on the bottom. Pre-bake the pie shell for single-crust pies.

Layered Raw Potato casseroles which cannot be stirred will not microwave evenly.

Pizza must be specially formulated for microwaving. Frozen pizza may be heated on a browning dish.

Stew

In conventional cooking, the time needed to cook a stew depends upon the type of meat used rather than the quantity. In microwaving, cooking time will vary according to the amount of meat and vegetables in the recipe. To estimate the time, look for a microwave recipe which contains a similar quantity of meat, vegetables and liquid. Cut the meat and vegetables into smaller pieces than you would conventionally. Use these guidelines to convert stews made with beef, pork, lamb or veal.

Microwaved stews do not evaporate as much as conventional ones, although the difference is not great because both are tightly covered. To maintain the consistency of the stew, you can reduce the liquid by about ⅓ or increase the amount of flour used to thicken the gravy.

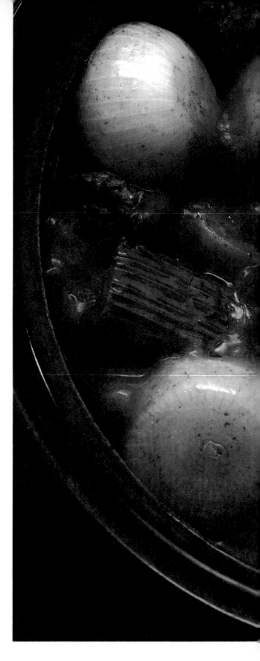

USE CHUCK CUT IN ¾ IN. CUBES.

OMIT

THINLY SLICED

CUT IN EIGHTHS.

Beef Stew

2 lbs. beef stew meat, cut in 1½-in. cubes
2 tablespoons shortening
2 cups hot water
1 medium onion, sliced
1 large bay leaf
1 tablespoon salt *—REDUCE*
1 teaspoon Worcestershire sauce
1 teaspoon sugar
¼ teaspoon pepper

⅛ teaspoon garlic powder
Dash ground cloves
6 carrots, peeled and quartered
4 potatoes, peeled and quartered
4 stalks celery, quartered lengthwise
1 lb. small white onions
3 tablespoons flour *—INCREASE*
⅓ cup cold water

Serves 6 to 8

5 QT. CASSEROLE   *OMIT*

In Dutch oven, brown meat in shortening. Add water, sliced onion, bay leaf, salt, Worcestershire sauce, sugar, pepper, garlic powder and cloves. Cover. Simmer for 1½ hours, stirring occasionally to prevent sticking. Remove bay leaf.

Add vegetables. Cover and simmer 30 to 45 minutes, or until meat and vegetables are tender.   *OMIT*

Blend flour into water, stir into stew. Stir constantly until bubbly. Cook 3 minutes more, stirring occasionally.

MICROWAVE AT HIGH. LET STAND 10 MINUTES.

MICROWAVE AT 50% (MEDIUM) STIRRING ONCE OR TWICE.

MICROWAVE AT HIGH 5 MINUTES. REDUCE POWER TO 50% (MEDIUM).

How to Microwave Stew

Select chuck rather than round for a more tender beef stew. Cut meat and vegetables into small, uniform pieces. Adjust the amount of liquid or flour slightly.

28

Converted Beef Stew

2 lbs. chuck, cut in ¾-in. cubes
2 cups hot water
1 medium onion, sliced
1 large bay leaf
2 teaspoons salt
1 teaspoon Worcestershire
   sauce
1 teaspoon sugar
¼ teaspoon pepper
⅛ teaspoon garlic powder
   Dash ground cloves
6 carrots, peeled and thinly
   sliced
4 potatoes, peeled and cut in
   eighths
4 stalks celery, quartered
   lengthwise
1 lb. small white onions
¼ cup flour
⅓ cup cold water

Serves 6 to 8

In 3-qt. casserole combine meat, water, sliced onion, bay leaf, salt, Worcestershire sauce, sugar, pepper, garlic powder and cloves. Cover.

Microwave at High 5 minutes. Reduce power to 50% (Medium). Microwave 40 minutes, stirring occasionally to prevent sticking. Remove bay leaf.

Add vegetables. Cover. Microwave 35 to 45 minutes, or until meat and vegetables are tender.

Blend flour into water, stir into stew. Microwave at High 3 to 4 minutes, or until bubbly, stirring once or twice. Let stand 10 minutes.

1¼ to 2½ hours.

Depending on size of vegetables, time will be longer if all ingredients are added at once.

Add vegetables at the beginning or part way through cooking as conventional recipe directs. Microwave at High 5 minutes. Reduce power to 50% (Medium).

Pot Roasts

Most pot roasts are made with beef, but these guidelines also apply to braised or casserole-roasted lamb, pork and veal.

Before microwaving a less tender beef roast, pierce it deeply on all surfaces with a fork so that steam and moisture can reach the interior of the meat. If your recipe specifies an amount of flour, dredge the meat as directed and then sprinkle on the remaining flour to help thicken the sauce. Browning is not necessary.

Some conventional recipes call for 4 or more cups of liquid to keep meat moist during cooking. This is not needed for microwaving; reduce the liquid to the amount desired for gravy.

Microwaving time for pot roast depends on the volume of meat, vegetables and liquid. Without the vegetables, this roast would take 5 to 10 minutes less time per pound. Standing time is essential to complete tenderizing and blend flavors.

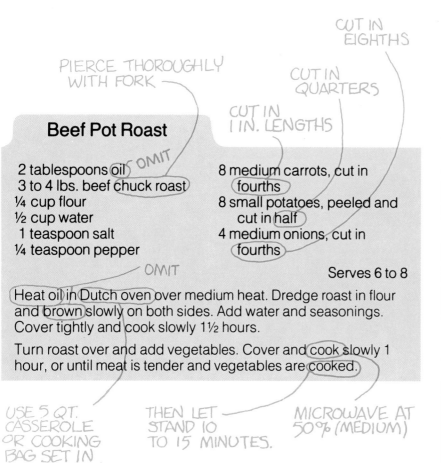

PIERCE THOROUGHLY WITH FORK

CUT IN EIGHTHS

CUT IN QUARTERS

CUT IN 1 IN. LENGTHS

Beef Pot Roast

2 tablespoons oil *OMIT*
3 to 4 lbs. beef chuck roast
¼ cup flour
½ cup water
1 teaspoon salt
¼ teaspoon pepper

8 medium carrots, cut in fourths
8 small potatoes, peeled and cut in half
4 medium onions, cut in fourths

Serves 6 to 8

OMIT

Heat oil in Dutch oven over medium heat. Dredge roast in flour and brown slowly on both sides. Add water and seasonings. Cover tightly and cook slowly 1½ hours.

Turn roast over and add vegetables. Cover and cook slowly 1 hour, or until meat is tender and vegetables are cooked.

USE 5 QT. CASSEROLE OR COOKING BAG SET IN BAKING DISH.

THEN LET STAND 10 TO 15 MINUTES.

MICROWAVE AT 50% (MEDIUM)

How to Microwave Pot Roast

Pierce meat on all sides with fork. Dredge in flour, if directed. Place meat in casserole or cooking bag.

Converted Beef Pot Roast

3 to 4 lbs. beef chuck roast
¼ cup flour
½ cup water
1 teaspoon salt
¼ teaspoon pepper
8 medium carrots, cut in 1-in. lengths
8 small potatoes, peeled and cut in fourths
4 medium onions, cut in eighths

Serves 6 to 8

Dredge roast in flour. Place roast in 5-qt. casserole or cooking bag set in baking dish. Sprinkle with remaining flour.

Add water and seasonings. Cover tightly or tie bag loosely with plastic strip cut from end of bag.

Microwave at 50% (Medium) 30 to 35 minutes per pound, turning roast over and adding vegetables after half the cooking time. Let stand 10 to 15 minutes.

25 to 40 minutes per lb.

Vegetables added after half of time. Time depends on cut of meat.

Add any flour remaining from the recipe and enough liquid for the amount of gravy desired. Cover casserole or seal bag.

Microwave at 50% (Medium), turning roast over and adding vegetables after half the cooking time. Let stand at least 10 minutes.

Less Tender Steaks

Turning over and rearranging meat during microwaving helps to cook it evenly. A recipe for Swiss steak which can be moved or stirred in its gravy is easier to adapt than one for layered Swiss steak. Follow these directions for pounding and microwaving the steak. Turn over or rearrange meat after half the cooking time.

Less tender beef should be microwaved at a lower power setting and then allowed to stand in order to make it tender. Pounding the beef tenderizes as well as flattens the meat.

In this recipe no change in ingredients was needed. We used the full amount of flour to help thicken the sauce as the meat cooked. Since browning was not necessary, we omitted the bacon drippings. A little bouquet sauce adds color to the gravy, if desired.

Time would be approximately the same for less meat, since it depends on meat tenderness rather than volume. If you make meat rolls with veal or pork, the method would be the same but cooking time would be shorter.

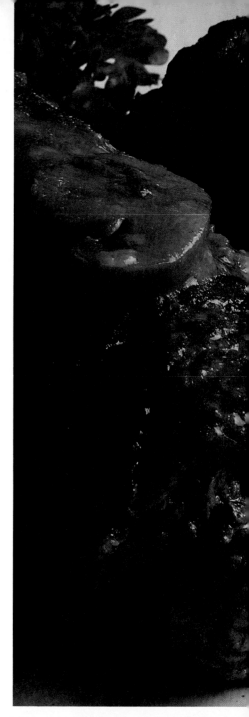

Beef Roll-Ups

ADD ¼ TSP. BOUQUET SAUCE FOR COLOR

2 to 2½ lb. round steak,
  ½-in. thick
6 slices bacon, cut in half
¼ cup finely chopped onion
¼ cup flour, divided
1¼ cups water, divided

1 can (4-oz.) mushroom stems
  and pieces, drained
1 teaspoon Worcestershire
  sauce
½ teaspoon salt
⅛ teaspoon pepper
⅛ teaspoon garlic powder

Serves 4

BE SURE TO USE ALL THE FLOUR

Cut round steak into 4 rectangles. Pound to ¼-in. thickness with the edge of a saucer or a meat mallet. *NOT NEEDED*

Fry bacon in 12-in. skillet over medium-high heat until limp. Place bacon on paper towels to drain. Reserve drippings in skillet.

Place 3 bacon halves and 1 tablespoon onion on each piece of round steak. Roll pieces and secure with wooden picks.

Dredge rolls in 2 tablespoons flour, then brown in bacon drippings over medium heat. Stir in 1 cup water, mushrooms, Worcestershire sauce and seasonings.

Cover. Simmer over low heat 1¼ to 1½ hours, or until beef is tender, turning rolls over after half the cooking time.

Combine ¼ cup water and 2 tablespoons flour. Stir gradually into sauce. Cook until thickened, stirring constantly.

USE PLASTIC WRAP *MICROWAVE AT 50% (MEDIUM)* *MICROWAVE AT HIGH STIRRING ONCE* *OMIT. PLACE ROLLS IN 8X8 IN. BAKING DISH. SPRINKLE WITH FLOUR REMAINING FROM DREDGING.*

MICROWAVE BETWEEN PAPER TOWELS.

How to Prepare Beef Roll-Ups

Pound meat with edge of saucer or meat mallet to flatten it and break down tough fibers.

Converted Beef Roll-Ups

2 to 2½ lb. round steak,
　½-in. thick
6 slices bacon, cut in half
¼ cup finely chopped onion
¼ cup flour, divided
1¼ cups water, divided
1 can (4-oz.) mushroom
　stems and pieces,
　drained
1 teaspoon Worcestershire
　sauce
½ teaspoon salt
⅛ teaspoon pepper
⅛ teaspoon garlic powder
¼ teaspoon bouquet sauce,
　optional

Serves 4

Cut round steak into 4 rectangles. Pound to ¼-in. thickness with the edge of a saucer or a meat mallet.

Place bacon on paper towels. Cover with paper towel. Microwave at High 3 to 5 minutes, or until partially cooked. Place 3 bacon halves and 1 tablespoon onion on each piece of round steak. Roll pieces and secure with wooden picks.

Dredge rolls in 2 tablespoons flour, then place in 8×8-in. baking dish. Sprinkle with any flour remaining from dredging. Stir in 1 cup water, mushrooms, Worcestershire sauce and seasonings.

Cover with plastic wrap. Microwave at 50% (Medium) 40 to 45 minutes, or until beef is tender, turning over and rearranging rolls after 20 minutes.

Combine ¼ cup water, 2 tablespoons flour and bouquet sauce, if desired. Stir gradually into sauce. Microwave at 50% (Medium) 5 to 7½ minutes, or until thickened, stirring once. Let stand, covered, 5 to 10 minutes.

40 to 55 minutes

2 to 2½ lbs. meat and 1 to 1½ cups gravy

Place stuffing on meat pieces, then roll up and secure with wooden picks.

Dredge rolls in flour. Arrange in baking dish and sprinkle with flour left over from dredging.

Tender Beef

Sautés of tender beef pieces, strips or chunks can be adapted to microwaving by using a browning utensil. For these dishes the beef is partially cooked, then finished in a sauce. Actual microwaving time depends on thickness of beef pieces and type of sauce.

Bourguignonne Sauce, made with wine, or Pizzaiola Sauce, made with tomatoes, can be finished at High power. Reduce power to 50% (Medium) when adding sauces made with cream or sour cream.

The only differences between the conventional and microwave versions of this sample recipe are the utensil, time and microwaving method. Notice that the melted butter and meat are stirred into the preheated browning dish together, then microwaved a minute or two. A microwaving method is also used to make the sauce.

...AND BUTTER MICROWAVE AT HIGH

MICROWAVE AT HIGH

PREHEAT 10-IN. BROWNING DISH

Beef Stroganoff

½ teaspoon salt
¼ cup flour, divided
1 lb. sirloin cut in thin strips
2 tablespoons butter or margarine
8 oz. mushrooms, sliced
1 medium onion, thinly sliced

1 clove garlic, minced
1 cup cool water
2 teaspoons instant beef bouillon granules
1 cup sour cream
½ cup whipping cream
2 tablespoons white wine

Serves 4 to 6

CUSTARD CUP

Combine salt and 1 tablespoon flour on wax paper. Toss meat with flour mixture until all flour is absorbed.

Melt 2 tablespoons butter in a large skillet over medium heat. Add meat, stirring until meat loses most of pink color. Stir in mushrooms, onions and garlic. Cook over medium heat until meat is cooked and vegetables are tender-crisp, stirring frequently. Remove from heat. With slotted spoon, remove meat and vegetables to platter.

In 2 cup measure, blend water, 3 tablespoons flour and bouillon. Over medium-high heat, slowly add bouillon mixture to pan drippings, stirring until mixture is smooth and thick.

Reduce heat to medium-low. Return meat and vegetables to sauce. Stir in remaining ingredients. Cook until heated through but not boiling, stirring constantly. Serve with rice, wild rice, or noodles.

MICROWAVE AT HIGH

ONCE OR TWICE

MICROWAVE AT 50% (MEDIUM)

How to Microwave Stroganoff

Stir melted butter and meat into preheated browning dish until sizzling stops. Microwave 1 to 2 minutes. Add vegetables and cook until tender.

Converted Beef Stroganoff

¼ cup flour, divided
½ teaspoon salt
1 lb. sirloin cut in thin strips
2 tablespoons butter or
    margarine
8 oz. mushrooms, sliced
1 medium onion, thinly sliced
1 clove garlic, minced
1 cup cool water
2 teaspoons instant beef
    bouillon granules
1 cup sour cream
½ cup whipping cream
2 tablespoons white wine

Serves 4 to 6

Combine 1 tablespoon flour and salt on wax paper. Toss meat with flour mixture until all flour is absorbed.

In a custard cup, microwave butter at High 20 to 45 seconds, or until melted.

Preheat 10-in. browning dish at High 5½ minutes. Add butter and meat, stirring until sizzling stops. Microwave at High 1 to 2 minutes, or until meat loses most of its pink color. Stir in mushrooms, onion and garlic. Microwave at High 3½ to 5½ minutes, or until vegetables are tender, stirring once or twice. With slotted spoon, remove meat and vegetables to platter.

Blend water, 3 tablespoons flour, and bouillon in 2 cup measure. Add to drippings in dish. Microwave at High 3 to 6 minutes, or until thickened, stirring once or twice during cooking.

Stir meat and vegetables into sauce. Thoroughly blend in sour cream, whipping cream and wine. Reduce power to 50% (Medium). Microwave 3 to 6 minutes or until heated through but not boiling, stirring once or twice.

Serve over rice, wild rice, or noodles.

10 to 20 minutes total

1 lb. sirloin cut in thin strips and 2 cups liquid

Remove meat and vegetables to platter. Microwave sauce at High until thickened, stirring once or twice.

Reduce power to 50% (Medium). Return meat and vegetables to dish. Blend in cream, sour cream and wine. Microwave until heated.

Stir-Fry

Microwaved stir-fries are even easier than conventional because there is practically no stirring. Be sure to have all ingredients ready before you start to cook.

Liquid may be added at the beginning or end of cooking, as conventional recipe directs. If a cornstarch mixture is stirred in at the end of cooking, microwave 1½ to 4 minutes at High to thicken the sauce.

For beef stir-fries, add meat and long-cooking vegetables at the same time, to avoid overcooking the meat. Pork, chicken and shellfish should be cooked first until they are done. Remove them from the browning dish while you microwave long-cooking vegetables until almost tender. Return them to the dish when you add the quick-cooking vegetables.

Total cooking time depends on the type of meat and vegetables used, the size of the pieces and the total quantity. When adapting a recipe for the first time, check for doneness frequently.

Sukiyaki

1 to 1½ lb. sirloin steak
2 tablespoons oil — REDUCE
⅓ cup soy sauce
¼ cup water
2 tablespoons sugar
2 stalks celery, thinly sliced
1 medium onion, thinly sliced
1 cup (1-in.) green onion
   pieces

1 can (5-oz.) bamboo shoots,
   drained
1 can (5-oz.) sliced water
   chestnuts, drained
2 cups fresh bean sprouts or
   1 can (1-lb.) drained
2 cups sliced fresh
   mushrooms

Serves 6 to 8

Cut sirloin into very thin slices across the grain, then into 1-in. strips. (Slicing is easier with partially frozen meat.) OMIT

Heat oil in large skillet or wok over high heat. Brown meat in oil 2 to 3 minutes. Combine soy sauce, water and sugar. Pour over meat. Bring to a boil. OMIT

Push meat to one side of skillet. Add celery, onion and bamboo shoots. Cook 5 to 7 minutes, or until vegetables are tender-crisp, turning vegetables occasionally.

OMIT
Push vegetables aside and add remaining ingredients. Cook 2 to 3 minutes or until thoroughly heated, stirring occasionally.

Serve with rice.

PREHEAT BROWNING
DISH AT HIGH...
THEN ADD OIL
AND MEAT.

MICROWAVE
AT HIGH
STIRRING
ONCE

MICROWAVE
AT HIGH
STIRRING
ONCE OR TWICE

Converted Sukiyaki

1 to 1½ lb. sirloin steak
⅓ cup soy sauce
¼ cup water
2 tablespoons sugar
1 tablespoon oil
2 stalks celery, thinly sliced
1 medium onion, thinly sliced
1 cup (1-in.) green onion pieces
1 can (5-oz.) bamboo shoots,
    drained
1 can (5-oz.) sliced water
    chestnuts, drained
2 cups fresh bean sprouts or 1
    can (1-lb.) drained
2 cups sliced fresh mushrooms

Serves 6 to 8

Cut sirloin into very thin slices across the grain, then into 1-in. strips. (Slicing is easier with partially frozen meat.)

Combine soy sauce, water and sugar in a 1 cup measure and set aside.

Preheat large browning dish 5 minutes at High. Add oil. Quickly stir in meat until sizzling stops.

Pour soy mixture over meat. Stir in celery, onion and bamboo shoots. Microwave at High 4 to 5½ minutes, or until vegetables are tender-crisp, stirring once.

Add remaining ingredients. Microwave at High 4 to 5½ minutes, or until mushrooms are tender and mixture is heated through, stirring once or twice.

6 to 20 minutes.

1 to 2 cups meat and 3 to 4 cups thinly sliced vegetables.

Meatloaf

Meatloaf is a balance between eggs, liquid and a filler like bread crumbs. Microwaving renders more fat from meat, and there is no hot, dry air in the oven to evaporate moisture, so the proportions of a conventional recipe must be adjusted. Use these guidelines to convert meatloaves made with uncooked beef, pork, lamb or veal.

You may use one of three methods shown below, depending on the type of filler required. To convert this conventional recipe, we selected the third method, which can be used with either dry or soft fillers.

If you are using frozen ground beef, defrost it partially until it can be worked. Mix the meatloaf while there are still some ice crystals in the meat. Actual microwaving time varies with the amount of moisture in the loaf; more moisture requires more time. Be guided by a similar microwave recipe, or check for doneness frequently.

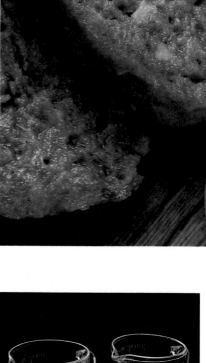

BREAD ATLEAST ONE DAY OLD WORKS BEST

DECREASE AND ADD ANOTHER EGG.

Meatloaf

1½ lbs. ground beef
3 slices white bread, torn into pieces
1 cup milk
1 egg

¼ cup chopped onion
1 tablespoon Worcestershire sauce
1½ teaspoons salt
¼ teaspoon pepper

Serves 6

Preheat oven to 350°.

Combine all ingredients. Spread in 9×5-in. ungreased loaf pan. Bake uncovered until done, about 1½ hours.

OMIT

MICROWAVE AT HIGH 13 TO 25 MINUTES ROTATING DISH AFTER HALF THE COOKING TIME. LET STAND 5 TO 10 MINUTES.

LOAF DISH

3 Ways to Adjust Moisture in Meatloaf

1. Increase dry filler, such as bread or cracker crumbs, quick rolled oats or crushed cereal by ¼ cup for 1½ pounds of meat.

2. Decrease liquid by half if the filler is soft bread crumbs.

3. Variation of Method 2. Substitute 1 egg for ¼ cup of the decreased liquid. Example: one egg plus ¼ cup milk equals ½ cup liquid, or half the amount in the conventional recipe above.

Converted Meatloaf

1½ lbs. ground beef
  3 slices white bread, torn into pieces
  ¼ cup milk
  2 eggs
  ¼ cup chopped onion
  1 tablespoon Worcestershire sauce
  1 teaspoon salt
  ⅛ teaspoon pepper

Serves 6

Combine all ingredients. Spread in 9×5-in. ungreased loaf dish.

Microwave at High 16 to 21 minutes, or until center is firm and has lost its pink color (internal temperature 145° to 150°), rotating dish after half the cooking time.

Let stand 5 to 10 minutes.

13 to 25 minutes

1½-lb. beef. Varies with moisture.

How to Microwave Meatloaf

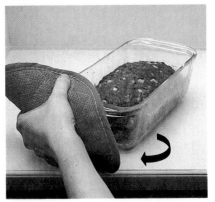

Microwave at High 13 to 25 minutes, depending on moisture content, rotating dish after half the cooking time.

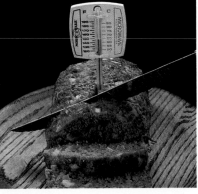

Remove from oven when center is firm and has lost its pink color (internal temperature 145° to 150°). Let stand 5 to 10 minutes.

Saucy meatloaf needs just enough sauce to cover top. Reduce the amount to ½ cup, or a maximum of 1 cup.

Meatballs

Meatballs may be converted in the same way as meatloaf, by adjusting the filler (bread or cracker crumbs), the liquid, or both. A binder, usually an egg, is needed to help meatballs hold together. If your recipe does not contain an egg, add one.

Meatballs may be microwaved with or without a sauce. It may be added at the beginning or part way through cooking. Sauces do not cook down in the short time needed to microwave them, so you should decrease the liquid by ¼, or increase the thickening.

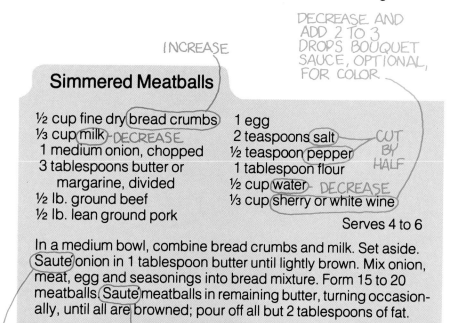

INCREASE

DECREASE AND ADD 2 TO 3 DROPS BOUQUET SAUCE, OPTIONAL, FOR COLOR

Simmered Meatballs

½ cup fine dry bread crumbs — *DECREASE*
⅓ cup milk — *DECREASE*
1 medium onion, chopped
3 tablespoons butter or margarine, divided
½ lb. ground beef
½ lb. lean ground pork

1 egg
2 teaspoons salt — *CUT BY HALF*
½ teaspoon pepper
1 tablespoon flour
½ cup water — *DECREASE*
⅓ cup sherry or white wine

Serves 4 to 6

In a medium bowl, combine bread crumbs and milk. Set aside. Saute onion in 1 tablespoon butter until lightly brown. Mix onion, meat, egg and seasonings into bread mixture. Form 15 to 20 meatballs. Saute meatballs in remaining butter, turning occasionally, until all are browned; pour off all but 2 tablespoons of fat.

Combine flour and water in 1 cup measure. Stir flour mixture and sherry into meatballs. Cook over low heat, stirring occasionally until sauce thickens and meatballs are cooked.

MICROWAVE AT HIGH IN A 12×8 IN. DISH, UNTIL ONION IS SOFT.

MICROWAVE MEATBALLS AT HIGH IN 12×8 IN. DISH, REARRANGING DURING COOKING.

MICROWAVE, COVERED WITH WAX PAPER, AT 50% (MEDIUM) STIRRING TWICE.

How to Microwave Meatballs

Microwave at High 7 to 10 minutes, until firm and no longer pink. Rearrange once or twice so least cooked ones are brought to outside of dish.

Sturdy sauces made with broth, water or tomatoes can be cooked rapidly at High. We reduced power to 50% (Medium) to give meatballs time to absorb flavor from the sauce.

Delicate sauces containing cream or sour cream should be microwaved at 50% (Medium) to prevent curdling.

Converted Simmered Meatballs

⅔ cup fine dry bread crumbs
¼ cup milk
1 medium onion, chopped
1 tablespoon butter or
   margarine
½ lb. ground beef
½ lb. ground pork
1 egg
1 teaspoon salt
¼ teaspoon pepper
1 tablespoon flour
⅓ cup water
¼ cup sherry
2 to 3 drops bouquet sauce,
   optional

Serves 4 to 6

In medium mixing bowl, combine bread crumbs and milk. Set aside. In 12×8-in. dish, microwave onion and butter at High 2½ to 4½ minutes or until onion is soft. Mix onion, meat, egg and seasonings into crumb mixture. Form 15 to 20 meatballs.

Arrange meatballs in 12×8-in. dish. Microwave at High 6½ to 9½ minutes, or until firm and no longer pink, rearranging once or twice during cooking, so least cooked meatballs are brought to outside of dish. Pour off all but 2 tablespoons of fat.

Combine flour and water in 1 cup measure. Stir flour mixture, sherry and bouquet sauce into meatballs. Cover with wax paper. Microwave at 50% (Medium) 5 to 8½ minutes, or until thickened, stirring once or twice during cooking.

5 to 13 minutes

1-lb. meat. Varies with moisture.

Serve miniature meatballs as appetizers, either plain or in a sauce. Convert and microwave your recipe as directed for main dish meatballs. Reduce the amount of sauce or gravy by ¼ to ½, so you have just enough to coat the meatballs.

Main Dish Meat Sauce

Meat sauces, such as chili, spaghetti sauce or sloppy joes adapt easily to microwaving. Reduce the liquid slightly, start microwaving at High, then cook uncovered at 50% (Medium) to develop flavor.

If you are in a hurry, substitute tomato sauce in recipes calling for canned tomatoes and microwave at High just until heated. These speedy sauces will not be as flavorful as simmered ones.

When converting a recipe for the first time, you may want to reduce salt and strong-flavored seasonings slightly, then add more to taste as needed. In the sample recipe, we made no changes in seasoning, since the amounts of salt, pepper and cayenne are small, and the quantity of chili powder depends on personal preference.

Chili

MICROWAVE AT HIGH

OMIT

1 lb. ground beef
1 medium onion, sliced
1 cup chopped celery
2 cans (10¾-oz.) tomato soup
1 can (16-oz.) kidney beans, undrained
½ cup water

REDUCE

1½ to 2 teaspoons chili powder
1 teaspoon brown sugar
1 teaspoon Worcestershire sauce
½ teaspoon salt
⅛ teaspoon pepper
⅛ teaspoon cayenne pepper

Makes about 2 quarts

Combine ground beef, onion and celery in 3-qt. casserole or Dutch oven. Cook uncovered over medium-high heat until meat is browned and vegetables are tender, stirring occasionally. Drain fat.

Stir in remaining ingredients. Bring to a boil. Cover, then simmer over low heat 55 to 60 minutes, stirring occasionally.

LOSES PINK COLOR

COVER. MICROWAVE AT HIGH 5 MINUTES. STIR

MICROWAVE UNCOVERED AT 50% (MEDIUM) STIRRING ATLEAST ONCE.

Converted Chili

1 lb. ground beef
1 medium onion, sliced
1 cup chopped celery
2 cans (10¾-oz.) tomato soup
1 can (16-oz.) kidney beans, undrained
¼ cup water
1½ to 2 teaspoons chili powder
1 teaspoon brown sugar
1 teaspoon Worcestershire sauce
½ teaspoon salt
⅛ teaspoon pepper
⅛ teaspoon cayenne pepper

Makes about 2 quarts

Combine ground beef, onion and celery in 3-qt. casserole. Microwave at High 6 to 9 minutes, or until meat is cooked and vegetables are tender. Drain fat and break up meat.

Stir in remaining ingredients. Cover. Microwave at High 5 minutes. Stir. Reduce power to 50% (Medium). Microwave uncovered 30 to 35 minutes, stirring twice.

How to Microwave Meat Sauce

Microwave meat and flavoring vegetables at High until meat loses its pink color. Drain fat and break up meat.

Reduce the liquid slightly. Add with remaining ingredients. Cover; microwave at High 5 minutes. Uncover; microwave at 50% (Medium).

10 to 35 minutes
1 lb. beef, 2 cups liquid

Longer time is needed for simmering

Casseroles: Sturdy Sauce

Sauces made with tomatoes, broth, soup or milk are sturdy and microwave well at High power. A minimum of stirring keeps the sauce smooth and distributes heat to speed cooking. When a sturdy sauce is combined with a meat which needs time to tenderize, it should be microwaved at 50% (Medium).

If your conventional casserole is baked uncovered, reduce the amount of liquid by ¼ to ½, since there will be little evaporation during microwaving. Check frequently and add more liquid if needed to achieve the desired consistency.

Covered casseroles, or those which contain very little liquid, will probably require no change. In the sample recipe we used the full amount of undiluted soup.

Hearty Sausage and Rice

1 lb. bulk sausage
1 medium onion, chopped
1 green pepper, chopped
2 cups cooked rice
1 can (10½-oz.) chicken with
  rice soup

1 can (8¾-oz.) corn, drained
½ teaspoon salt
¼ teaspoon pepper

Serves 4 to 6

OMIT

Preheat oven to 350°.   *2 QT. CASSEROLE*

Crumble sausage into medium skillet. Add onion and green pepper. Cook over medium heat until sausage is set and vegetables are tender. Drain.

In 2-qt. oven-proof casserole, combine sausage and remaining ingredients. Cover. Bake 35 to 45 minutes, or until bubbly.

MICROWAVE AT HIGH STIRRING ONCE.

Converted Hearty Sausage and Rice

1 lb. bulk sausage
1 medium onion, chopped
1 green pepper, chopped
2 cups cooked rice
1 can (10½-oz.) chicken with
  rice soup

1 can (8¾-oz.) corn, drained
½ teaspoon salt
¼ teaspoon pepper

Serves 4 to 6

Crumble sausage into 2-qt. casserole. Add onion and green pepper. Cover. Microwave at High 4½ to 7½ minutes, or until sausage is set and vegetables are tender, stirring once. Drain.

Stir in remaining ingredients. Cover. Microwave at High 6½ to 9 minutes, or until heated through (140° to 150°), stirring once.

6 to 13 minutes
1½ to 2-qt. casserole
Pre-cooked ingredients

How to Adapt Casseroles

Select power setting suitable for the type of meat used.

with Sturdy Sauce

Reduce liquid by ¼ to ½ if your conventional recipe is very saucy or baked uncovered.

Covered or very dry casseroles require no change in liquid.

Stir once or twice during micro-waving for even cooking.

Casseroles: Delicate Sauce

Sauces made with cream or sour cream should be microwaved at 50% (Medium) because they are sensitive to over-heating. This is also true of layered casseroles containing cream cheese and cottage cheese, which cannot be stirred to distribute heat.

In this sample recipe, the principal change was in the order in which ingredients were added. By stirring the cheese mixture and adding the sour cream toward the end of cooking, we were able to use High power for most of the time. If the cream were added at the beginning, the casserole would be microwaved at 50% (Medium) and would take twice the time.

The tomato slices would overcook if microwaved for the total time, so we added them part way through. When the casserole was hot, we stirred in the sour cream, sprinkled on the paprika and reduced the power to 50% (Medium) for a brief final heating.

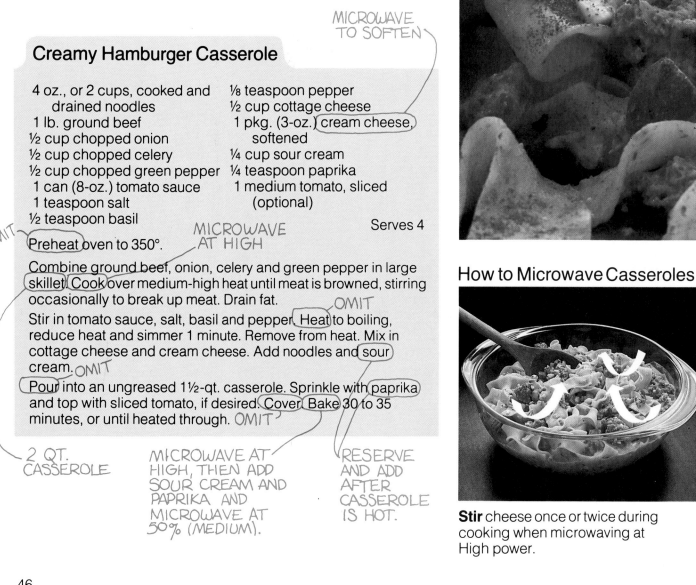

Creamy Hamburger Casserole

MICROWAVE TO SOFTEN

4 oz., or 2 cups, cooked and drained noodles
1 lb. ground beef
½ cup chopped onion
½ cup chopped celery
½ cup chopped green pepper
1 can (8-oz.) tomato sauce
1 teaspoon salt
½ teaspoon basil

⅛ teaspoon pepper
½ cup cottage cheese
1 pkg. (3-oz.) cream cheese, softened
¼ cup sour cream
¼ teaspoon paprika
1 medium tomato, sliced (optional)

Serves 4

OMIT Preheat oven to 350°.

MICROWAVE AT HIGH

Combine ground beef, onion, celery and green pepper in large skillet. Cook over medium-high heat until meat is browned, stirring occasionally to break up meat. Drain fat.

Stir in tomato sauce, salt, basil and pepper. *OMIT* Heat to boiling, reduce heat and simmer 1 minute. Remove from heat. Mix in cottage cheese and cream cheese. Add noodles and sour cream. *OMIT*

Pour into an ungreased 1½-qt. casserole. Sprinkle with paprika and top with sliced tomato, if desired. Cover. Bake 30 to 35 minutes, or until heated through. *OMIT*

2 QT. CASSEROLE

MICROWAVE AT HIGH, THEN ADD SOUR CREAM AND PAPRIKA AND MICROWAVE AT 50% (MEDIUM).

RESERVE AND ADD AFTER CASSEROLE IS HOT.

How to Microwave Casseroles

Stir cheese once or twice during cooking when microwaving at High power.

Converted Creamy Hamburger Casserole

4 oz., or 2 cups, cooked and
    drained noodles
1 pkg. (3-oz.) cream cheese,
    softened
1 lb. ground beef
½ cup chopped onion
½ cup chopped celery
½ cup chopped green pepper
1 can (8-oz.) tomato sauce
½ cup cottage cheese
1 teaspoon salt
½ teaspoon basil
⅛ teaspoon pepper
1 medium tomato, sliced
    (optional)
¼ cup sour cream
¼ teaspoon paprika

Serves 4

In small bowl, soften cream cheese at High 15 to 20 seconds. Set aside.

In 2-qt. casserole combine ground beef, onion, celery and green pepper. Microwave at High 4 to 6 minutes, or until meat is cooked and vegetables are tender. Stir to break up meat; drain.

Stir in tomato sauce, cottage cheese, cream cheese, salt, basil, pepper and noodles. Microwave at High 4 minutes. Stir.

Top with sliced tomato, if desired. Microwave at High 4 to 7 minutes, uncovered, or until hot and bubbly. Place sliced tomato to one side. Stir in sour cream. Sprinkle with paprika and rearrange tomato slices on top.

Microwave at 50% (Medium) 2 to 3 minutes, or until heated through.

9 to 18 minutes.

2-qt. casserole

Containing Delicate Foods

Reduce power to 50% (Medium) to heat cream or sour cream.

Casseroles: Cubed Cooked Meat, Raw Potatoes

When cooked meat is combined with raw potatoes it is important to cut the meat in ¾-in. cubes and slice the potatoes thinly. Sliced meat would require a lower power setting. If the cubes are well covered with sauce, they can be heated at High for the time needed to cook thinly sliced potatoes. Stirring also helps prevent overcooking so that High can be used.

Microwaving simplified the preparation of this scalloped potato casserole. We were able to make the sauce right in the final baking dish and stir in, rather than layer, the ham and potatoes. If you wish to use a packaged mix, soak the dehydrated potatoes in the sauce for 20 minutes before adding the ham, or reduce liquid by ¾ cup.

Because microwaving retains more moisture than oven baking, we substituted wax paper for the foil. The paper held in sufficient moisture and speeded cooking. Plastic wrap holds in too much steam and thins the sauce.

Ham & Scalloped Potatoes

USE 12×8 IN. DISH

3 tablespoons butter or
  margarine
¼ cup finely chopped onion
3 tablespoons flour
½ teaspoon salt
½ teaspoon dry mustard

⅛ teaspoon pepper
1½ cups milk
3 cups cubed cooked ham
5 cups peeled and thinly
  sliced potatoes

Serves 4 to 6

OMIT ~~Preheat~~ oven to 350°.

MICROWAVE (AT HIGH *OMIT*

Melt butter in 2-qt. saucepan over medium heat. Stir in onion, flour, salt, dry mustard and pepper. Cook over medium heat until mixture is bubbly, stirring constantly. Gradually stir in milk. Cook until mixture is thickened, stirring constantly.

Place ham cubes in 12×8-in. baking dish. Arrange potatoes over ham. Pour sauce on top, spreading to cover potatoes. Cover with

WAX PAPER foil and bake 30 minutes.

Stir. Bake, uncovered, 45 to 60 minutes, or until sauce is thickened and potatoes are tender.

MICROWAVE AT HIGH STIRRING 3 OR 4 TIMES

STIR BEFORE SERVING

MICROWAVE AT HIGH STIRRING EVERY 2 MINUTES.

STIR HAM AND POTATOES INTO SAUCE.

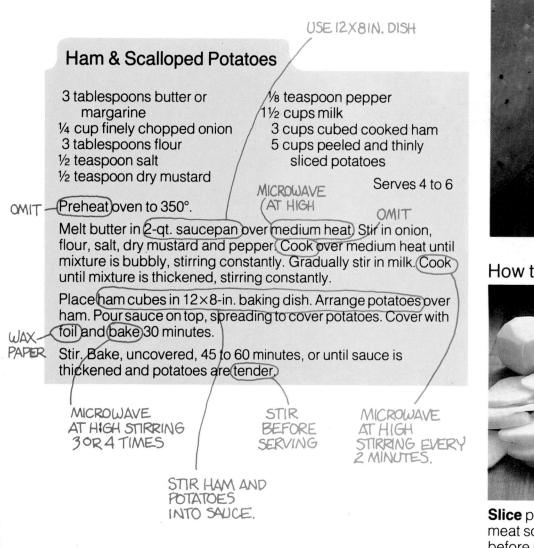

How to Adapt Casseroles

Slice potatoes thinly and cube meat so it will not overcook before potatoes are tender.

Converted Ham & Scalloped Potatoes

3 tablespoons butter or
  margarine
¼ cup finely chopped onion
3 tablespoons flour
½ teaspoon salt
½ teaspoon dry mustard
⅛ teaspoon pepper
1½ cups milk
3 cups cubed cooked ham
5 cups peeled and thinly
  sliced potatoes

Serves 4 to 6

Place butter in 12×8-in. dish; microwave at High 45 seconds to 1 minute, or until melted. Stir in onion, flour, salt, dry mustard and pepper. Blend in milk. Microwave at High 5 to 7 minutes, or until thickened, stirring every 2 minutes.

Mix in ham and potatoes, stirring to coat with sauce. Cover with wax paper. Microwave at High 17 to 22 minutes, or until potatoes are tender, stirring 3 or 4 times during cooking. Stir before serving.

15 to 27 minutes

3 cups cooked meat. 5 cups thin potatoes. Varies with amount of sauce.

with Raw Potatoes

Stir 3 or 4 times during microwaving. Avoid layered casseroles, which may cook unevenly.

Soak potatoes in sauce 20 minutes before microwaving or reduce water by ¾ cup when using a package mix.

Casseroles:
Uncooked Ground Meat and Raw Potatoes

This casserole illustrates what to look for when selecting a recipe for microwave conversion. The conventional cooking method adapts well to microwaving; the main ingredients (ground beef, potatoes and broth) all microwave well at High power with a minimum of attention. Although the ground beef will be cooked before the potatoes, the soup will prevent overcooking.

The only changes made in ingredients were to slice the potatoes thinly so they would cook quickly, to reduce the salt and to omit the water, since potatoes microwave in their own natural moisture. This recipe also demonstrates two advantages of microwaving: fewer dirty dishes and greatly reduced cooking time.

Converted Hamburger & Potato Casserole

1 lb. ground beef
5 medium potatoes, peeled and thinly sliced
1 can (10½-oz.) vegetable beef soup
½ teaspoon salt
1 can (3-oz.) French fried onion rings

Serves 4 to 6

Crumble hamburger in 12×8-in. baking dish. Microwave at High 4 to 6 minutes, or until meat loses most of its pink color. Break up and drain.

Stir in potatoes, soup and salt. Cover with wax paper. Microwave at High 14 to 18 minutes, or until potatoes are tender and liquid is absorbed, stirring after half the cooking time.

Stir mixture and sprinkle onion rings over top. Microwave, uncovered, at High 1½ to 3 minutes, or until heated through.

13 to 22 minutes

1 lb. hamburger, cooked, 5 medium potatoes thinly sliced. Varies with amount of other ingredients and sauce.

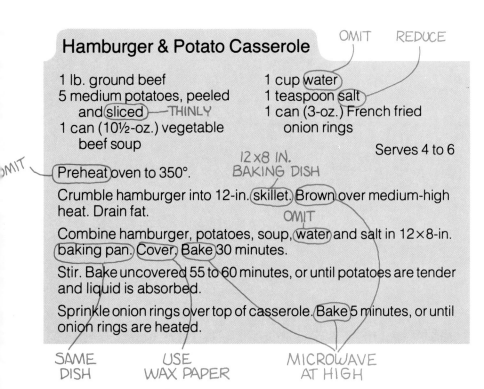

Hamburger & Potato Casserole

OMIT   REDUCE

1 lb. ground beef
5 medium potatoes, peeled and (sliced) —THINLY
1 can (10½-oz.) vegetable beef soup
1 cup (water)
1 teaspoon (salt)
1 can (3-oz.) French fried onion rings

Serves 4 to 6

OMIT

(Preheat) oven to 350°.

12 X 8 IN. BAKING DISH

Crumble hamburger into 12-in. (skillet.) (Brown) over medium-high heat. Drain fat.

OMIT

Combine hamburger, potatoes, soup, (water) and salt in 12×8-in. (baking pan.) (Cover.) (Bake) 30 minutes.

Stir. Bake uncovered 55 to 60 minutes, or until potatoes are tender and liquid is absorbed.

Sprinkle onion rings over top of casserole. (Bake 5 minutes, or until onion rings are heated.

SAME DISH   USE WAX PAPER   MICROWAVE AT HIGH

Why This is a Good Recipe for Microwave

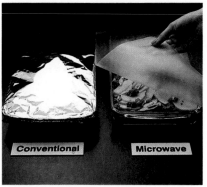

Conventional dish is covered for part of time, indicating need for steam. Moist dishes adapt well for microwaving.

Ingredients in this recipe microwave well at High power. Thinly sliced potatoes take longer to cook, but the ground beef and soup are sturdy and can be added at the start of microwaving.

How to Convert Pork Chops on Rice

Substitute twice the amount of quick-cooking rice for raw or converted rice, to get the same number of servings.

Reduce liquid by ¼, or use the amount recommended on the rice package.

Casseroles: Raw or Cooked Meat and Rice

Most meat and rice combinations are easier to convert if you use quick-cooking rice, which tenderizes in the short time needed to microwave the meat. See page 66 if you wish to use raw long-grain rice. Since quick-cooking rice is already partially rehydrated, you must double the amount of rice and reduce the liquid to obtain the same number of servings. For this recipe we cut the liquid by approximately ¼. Rather than use part of a can of chicken broth, we substituted water and bouillon granules.

We brushed the chops with a browning mixture to give them an attractive appearance. This step can be omitted if your recipe contains a colorful sauce. Microwaving time for your casserole will depend on the amount and type of meat used.

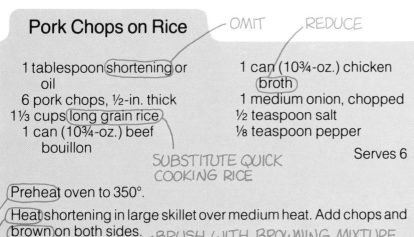

Pork Chops on Rice

OMIT *REDUCE*

1 tablespoon shortening or oil
6 pork chops, ½-in. thick
1⅓ cups long grain rice
1 can (10¾-oz.) beef bouillon

1 can (10¾-oz.) chicken broth
1 medium onion, chopped
½ teaspoon salt
⅛ teaspoon pepper

Serves 6

SUBSTITUTE QUICK COOKING RICE

Preheat oven to 350°.

Heat shortening in large skillet over medium heat. Add chops and brown on both sides. *BRUSH WITH BROWNING MIXTURE*

While chops are browning, combine remaining ingredients in 12×8-in. baking pan or dish. Top with browned chops and cover with foil. Bake 1 hour, or until chops are done and rice has absorbed all moisture.

OMIT   *PLASTIC WRAP*   *MICROWAVE AT HIGH 5 MINUTES THEN AT 50% (MEDIUM)*

Converted Pork Chops on Rice

2⅔ cups quick cooking rice
1 can (10¾-oz.) beef bouillon
½ cup water
1 medium onion, finely chopped
1 teaspoon instant chicken bouillon granules
½ teaspoon salt
⅛ teaspoon pepper
6 pork chops, ½-in. thick
1 teaspoon water
1 teaspoon bouquet sauce

Serves 6

Combine all ingredients except pork chops, 1 teaspoon water and bouquet sauce, in 12×8-in. baking dish. Arrange chops over rice with meatiest portions to outside of dish. Combine water and bouquet sauce in small bowl. Brush mixture on chops. Cover with plastic wrap.

Microwave at High 5 minutes. Reduce power to 50% (Medium). Microwave 15 to 20 minutes, or until chops are done and rice has absorbed moisture, rearranging chops after half the cooking time.

14 to 25 minutes

6 pork chops ½-in. thick and quick-cooking rice. Thicker liquid (soup) would take longer.

Arrange chops over rice; meatiest portions to outside of dish.

Brush chops with diluted bouquet sauce for color.

Casseroles: Cooked Meat and Uncooked Pasta

Use this sample recipe as a guide to converting casseroles which contain a similar amount of canned or cooked meat, chicken or fish.

Macaroni needs steam to tenderize. A tight cover is essential. If your casserole has a cover, place it over plastic wrap for a tight seal. To stir, use pot holders and lift cover away from you to avoid burns.

We started the casserole at High, then reduced the power to 50% (Medium) to give the macaroni time to rehydrate without overheating the other ingredients. Cooking time depends on the size of the macaroni, larger pasta takes more time.

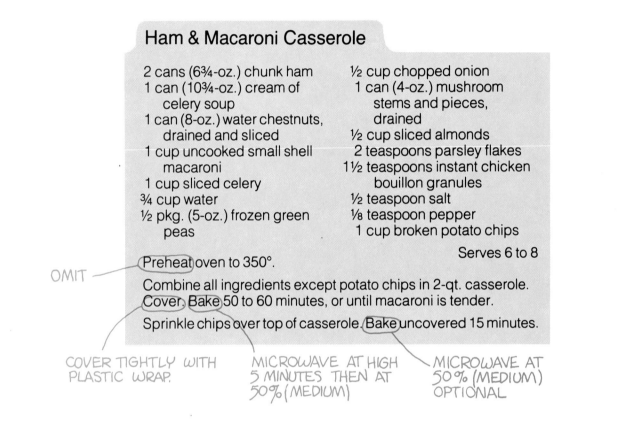

Ham & Macaroni Casserole

2 cans (6¾-oz.) chunk ham
1 can (10¾-oz.) cream of
    celery soup
1 can (8-oz.) water chestnuts,
    drained and sliced
1 cup uncooked small shell
    macaroni
1 cup sliced celery
¾ cup water
½ pkg. (5-oz.) frozen green
    peas

½ cup chopped onion
1 can (4-oz.) mushroom
    stems and pieces,
    drained
½ cup sliced almonds
2 teaspoons parsley flakes
1½ teaspoons instant chicken
    bouillon granules
½ teaspoon salt
⅛ teaspoon pepper
1 cup broken potato chips

Serves 6 to 8

Preheat oven to 350°.   *— OMIT*

Combine all ingredients except potato chips in 2-qt. casserole. Cover. Bake 50 to 60 minutes, or until macaroni is tender.

Sprinkle chips over top of casserole. Bake uncovered 15 minutes.

COVER TIGHTLY WITH PLASTIC WRAP.

MICROWAVE AT HIGH 5 MINUTES THEN AT 50% (MEDIUM)

MICROWAVE AT 50% (MEDIUM) OPTIONAL

How to Adapt Raw Pasta Casserole

Use full amount of liquid. Pasta will absorb it.

Cover dish very tightly to produce plenty of steam.

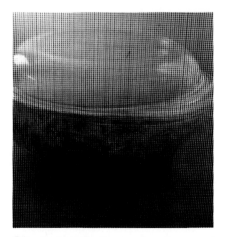

Start at High, then microwave at 50% (Medium) to allow pasta enought time to soften.

Converted Ham & Macaroni Casserole

2 cans (6¾-oz.) chunk ham
1 can (10¾-oz.) cream of
    celery soup
1 can (8-oz.) water chestnuts,
    drained and sliced
1 cup uncooked small shell
    macaroni*
1 cup sliced celery
¾ cup water
½ pkg. (5-oz.) frozen green
    peas
½ cup chopped onion
1 can (4-oz.) mushroom stems
    and pieces, drained
½ cup sliced almonds
2 teaspoons parsley flakes
1½ teaspoons instant chicken
    bouillon granules
½ teaspoon salt
⅛ teaspoon pepper
1 cup broken potato chips

Serves 6 to 8

Combine all ingredients except
potato chips in 2-qt. casserole.
Cover tightly. Microwave at High
3 minutes. Reduce power to
50% (Medium). Microwave 13 to
16½ minutes, or until macaroni
is tender, stirring once or twice.

Sprinkle chips over top of
casserole. Microwave 1 to 2
minutes to heat chips, if desired.

*For elbow macaroni microwave
8 to 12 minutes longer.

16 to 30 minutes

Similar amount of liquid
and pasta. Varies with size
of pasta.

Casseroles: Layered

Layered casseroles should be rotated ¼ or ½ turn during microwaving. Reduce the power level to 50% (Medium) even when all ingredients microwave well at High power, since they cannot be stirred to distribute heat. The lower power level prevents overcooking the edges before the center is done. Changes in liquid and seasonings are similar to stirable casseroles and depend on the type of ingredients used.

In conventional cooking, lasagna noodles should be rinsed well in cool water to make them easy to handle and prevent sticking to the towel on which they are drained. Microwaved noodles tend to be starchy because they are cooked in a minimum of water. Since the starch can be washed away, we microwaved the noodles and let them drain while we cooked the sauce which was started at High, then microwaved at 50% (Medium) to reduce liquid and develop flavor.

PARTIALLY DRAINED

MICROWAVE AT HIGH, UNTIL MEAT LOSES PINK COLOR, STIRRING ONCE.

Lasagna

1 lb. ground beef
1 medium onion, chopped
1 clove garlic, minced
1 can (16-oz.) whole tomatoes
1 can (15-oz.) tomato sauce
3 tablespoons parsley flakes, divided
1½ teaspoons salt, divided
1 teaspoon oregano
1 teaspoon basil   *REDUCE*

1 teaspoon brown sugar
9 uncooked lasagna noodles (8-oz.)
1 carton (16-oz.) ricotta or large curd cottage cheese
2 eggs
½ cup Parmesan cheese, divided
¼ teaspoon pepper
2 cups shredded Mozzarella cheese

2 QT. CASSEROLE   Serves 8

Combine ground beef, onion and garlic in 12-in. skillet. Cook over medium heat until ground beef is browned, stirring occasionally. Drain.

Stir in tomatoes, tomato sauce, 2 tablespoons parsley flakes, ½ teaspoon salt, oregano, basil and brown sugar. Simmer, uncovered, over medium-low heat 1 to 1¼ hours, or until mixture is thickened. *MICROWAVE NOODLES FIRST IN 12X8 IN. DISH*

Cook noodles as directed on package. Rinse well in cool water; spread on towels to drain. Preheat oven to 350°. *OMIT*

In medium bowl mix ricotta cheese, eggs, ¼ cup Parmesan cheese, 1 tablespoon parsley flakes, 1 teaspoon salt and pepper.

In 12×8-in. baking pan layer ⅓ each of the noodles, ricotta mixture, sauce and Mozzarella cheese. Repeat twice. Sprinkle with ¼ cup Parmesan cheese. *DISH*

Bake uncovered 40 to 50 minutes, or until bubbly. Let stand 15 minutes to set before cutting.

MICROWAVE AT 50% (MEDIUM) ROTATING DISH ½ TURN AFTER HALF COOKING TIME.

MICROWAVE AT HIGH, THEN 50% (MEDIUM) STIRRING 2 OR 3 TIMES.

How to Microwave Noodles

Measure ½ teaspoon salt, 1 tablespoon oil and 5 cups very hot tap water into a 12×8-in. baking dish. Cover tightly with plastic wrap. Microwave at High 5 to 8 minutes, or until water boils.

Converted Lasagna

9 uncooked lasagna noodles
1 lb. ground beef
1 medium onion, chopped
1 clove garlic, minced
1 can (16-oz.) tomatoes, drain
   all but ⅓ cup juice
1 can (15-oz.) tomato sauce
3 tablespoons parsley flakes,
   divided
1 teaspoon salt, divided
1 teaspoon oregano
1 teaspoon basil
1 teaspoon brown sugar
1 carton (16-oz.) ricotta or
   large curd cottage cheese
2 eggs
½ cup Parmesan cheese,
   divided
¼ teaspoon pepper
2 cups shredded Mozzarella

Serves 8

Microwave noodles according to photo directions.

Combine ground beef, onion and garlic in 2-qt. casserole. Microwave at High 4½ to 7½ minutes, or until meat loses its pink color, stirring once. Drain.

Stir in tomatoes, tomato sauce, 2 tablespoons parsley flakes, ½ teaspoon salt, oregano, basil and brown sugar. Microwave at High 5 minutes, reduce power to 50% (Medium). Microwave 30 to 40 miunutes, or until thickened, stirring two or three times.

In medium bowl mix ricotta, eggs, ¼ cup Parmesan, 1 tablespoon parsley flakes, ½ teaspoon salt and pepper. In 12×8-in. baking dish layer ⅓ each of the noodles, ricotta mixture, sauce and Mozzarella. Repeat twice. Sprinkle with ¼ cup Parmesan.

Microwave at 50% (Medium) 20 to 30 minutes, or until bubbly, rotating dish ½ turn, after half the cooking time. Let stand 15 minutes to set before cutting.

15 to 40 minutes
12×8-in. lasagna dish.
Depending on similar amount and temperature of sauce.

for Lasagna

Add noodles. Cover tightly. Microwave at High 5½ to 8 minutes, or until lasagna are tender but still very firm, rearranging once after half the cooking time.

Rinse well under cool water to remove starch. Spread on towels to drain.

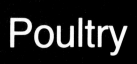

Adapting Poultry

Poultry is an excellent choice for microwaving. Dark meat is less likely to be pink toward the bone; white meat remains more moist than conventionally cooked.

Most poultry can be microwaved at High power in ½ to ⅓ the conventional cooking time. Use 50% (Medium) power for delicate sauces containing cream or eggs and large pieces, such as a whole chicken or turkey parts.

Stewing hens can be microwaved at 50% (Medium), but cooking time will be almost as long as conventional and the skin will not tenderize. We recommend substituting a broiler-fryer in chicken stews.

Liquid. The Guidelines for Meat and Main Dishes, page 26, apply to poultry as well. Reduce liquid by ⅓ to ½, unless it is needed to rehydrate rice or pasta. Use a little less seasoning and add more to taste after microwaving.

Fat. Microwaving renders more fat from chicken than conventional cooking, an advantage for dieters who are cutting calories and cholesterol. Drain fat from chicken before adding other ingredients or finishing a sauce.

Since most chicken fat is in or under the skin, you can reduce fat even more by skinning the chicken before microwaving. If the chicken is not skinned, use a colorful sauce or brush the skin with soy sauce or diluted bouquet sauce for a browned appearance.

Crumb Coatings. This book does not give directions for crumb-coated chicken because no converting is necessary. Use your favorite coating recipe, arrange 2½ to 3 lbs. of chicken pieces on a rack and microwave at High 18 to 25 minutes. Rearrange, but don't turn the chicken over after the first 10 minutes.

Casseroles. Most cooks have a file of favorite recipes for cooked chicken and turkey. With a microwave oven you don't have to wait until you have leftovers. Microwave chicken parts in a covered dish. It takes 2½ to 4½ minutes for a single piece or 5½ to 7½ minutes per pound.

Stuffings and Dressings. Use the microwave oven to prepare your favorite stuffings for poultry. You can saute' vegetables, toast nuts or cook sausage right in the bowl you will use to mix the dressing for easy clean-up.

Times will depend on the amount and type of ingredients. Consult a microwave sausage cooking chart, or a casserole recipe from this book which gives times for a similar amount of meat or chopped vegetables.

How to Brown Microwave Poultry

Plain microwaved chicken is light gold in color. It appears cooked, but skin does not crisp.

Sprinkle chicken pieces with dry soup or gravy mixes to add both flavor and color.

Brush chicken with melted butter, sprinkle with paprika.

Pour off fat from chicken before finishing a sauce. Microwaving extracts more fat than conventional cooking.

Reduce liquid by ⅓ to ½. Add more during cooking, if needed. Liquids do not evaporate in the short time required to cook chicken.

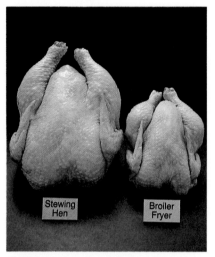

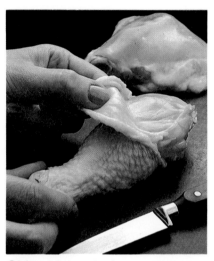

Some Things That Don't Work and Why

Deep-fried chicken cannot be microwaved because the fat reaches very high temperatures and can cause burns, however, you may use the microwave oven to reheat fried chicken.

Oven-broiled Chicken cannot be achieved by microwaving because it will not have a crisp, browned surface.

Select a broiler-fryer rather than a stewing hen to take full advantage of microwave speed.

Skin chicken before cooking to eliminate excess fat. Wash unskinned chicken thoroughly.

Make a colorful sauce from your own recipe or use bottled barbecue, soy or teriyaki sauce.

Rub mixture of equal parts of melted butter and bouquet sauce into well-dried chicken skin.

Dip chicken in melted butter or beaten egg, then homemade or packaged crumb mixture.

Chicken: Pieces in Delicate Sauce

Chicken pieces microwave well at High power, but delicate sauces containing cream, sour cream or eggs require a lower setting to prevent overheating. In conventional cooking, the chicken is usually browned first, which partially cooks it and shortens the time needed to cook it in sauce. While browning is not needed in microwaving, partial cooking can be achieved by starting the chicken at High before the sauce is added.

If the chicken were dredged in flour before this initial cooking, the surface would become pasty; so we added the full amount of flour to the sauce. Since the conventional recipe is cooked covered, there is little evaporation. It was not necessary to reduce the amount of liquid in order to achieve the same sauce consistency with microwaving.

Chicken Imperial

2 whole large chicken breasts, halved, skinned
2 tablespoons all-purpose flour
5 tablespoons butter or margarine

8 oz. fresh mushrooms, sliced
¼ cup chopped onion
1 cup whipping cream
¼ cup white wine
1 teaspoon salt
Dash pepper

Serves 4

Dredge chicken in flour. Melt butter over medium heat in 10-in. skillet. Brown chicken lightly on both sides; remove from skillet.

Saute mushrooms and onion in butter until tender, stirring frequently. Stir in cream, wine, salt and pepper. Return chicken to skillet. Simmer chicken, covered, over low heat 20 to 25 minutes, or until tender. Serve with sauce.

NOTE: For thicker sauce: Remove chicken to warm platter. In 1 cup measure, blend 1 tablespoon flour and 2 tablespoons water. Stir into cream mixture. Cook over medium-low heat, stirring constantly, until mixture thickens. Serve sauce over chicken.

Handwritten annotations:
REDUCE
OMIT
ADD FLOUR TO SAUCE
12 X 8 IN. DISH
OMIT
PLASTIC WRAP
MICROWAVE AT HIGH THEN ADD CHICKEN, COVER AND MICROWAVE 5 MINUTES ROTATING DISH ONCE
MICROWAVE AT 50% (MEDIUM) STIRRING ONCE

How to Adapt Chicken in Delicate Sauce

Start the chicken and flavoring vegetables at High power. Cover dish and rotate after 3 minutes.

Spoon sauce ingredients over chicken. Cover with vented plastic wrap. Microwave at 50% (Medium) until chicken is tender, rearranging after half the cooking time.

Converted Chicken Imperial

2 tablespoons butter or
    margarine
8 oz. fresh mushrooms, sliced
¼ cup chopped onion
2 whole large chicken breasts,
    halved, skinned
2 tablespoons all-purpose flour
¼ cup white wine
1 cup whipping cream
1 teaspoon salt
    Dash pepper

Serves 4

In 12×8-in. dish, combine butter, mushrooms and onions. Cover with plastic wrap. Microwave at High 3 to 5 minutes, or until vegetables are tender. Add chicken breasts and cover. Microwave 5 minutes, rotating dish once.

In 2 cup measure, blend flour and wine. Stir in cream, salt and pepper. Remove chicken from dish. Stir cream mixture into vegetables. Place chicken in dish, spoon cream mixture over chicken. Cover with plastic wrap. Reduce power to 50% (Medium). Microwave 9 to 14 minutes, or until chicken is tender and no longer pink, rearranging once.

NOTE: For thicker gravy: Remove chicken to platter. In 1 cup measure, blend 2 tablespoons water and 1 tablespoon flour. Stir into cream mixture. Microwave at 50% (Medium) 2 to 5 minutes, or until thickened, stirring once.

7 to 20 minutes

2 whole chicken breasts. 1½ cups sauce

Chicken: Pieces in Sturdy Sauce

Chicken and durable sauces such as barbecue, tomato, soy or condensed soup, both microwave well at High power. While your conventional recipe may call for a cover, wax paper is sufficient to keep the chicken moist during microwaving.

If your conventional recipe calls for more than a cup of sauce, reduce the amount by ¼ to ½. All you need is enough sauce to cover the chicken. No change was needed in the sample recipe. Add the sauce at the beginning or part way through cooking as your conventional recipe directs.

Converted Barbecue Chicken

¾ cup chili sauce or catsup
3 tablespoons brown sugar
1 tablespoon vinegar or lemon juice
1 tablespoon instant minced onion
1 teaspoon mustard
4 to 5 drops liquid smoke, optional
2 to 3 lb. cut up fryer

Serves 4 to 6

Combine all ingredients except chicken in 2 cup measure. Place chicken skin side down in 12×8-in. baking dish. Cover with half the sauce. Cover loosely with wax paper. Microwave at High 3 minutes per lb. Drain fat.

Rearrange chicken skin side up, so that less cooked areas are to outside of dish. Spread with remaining sauce. Cover with wax paper. Microwave at High 2½ to 4½ minutes per lb., or until chicken is fork tender.

NOTE: Skin may be removed if desired.

5 to 9 minutes per lb.

Depending on amount and temperature of chicken and sauce.

Barbecue Chicken

¾ cup chili sauce or catsup
3 tablespoons brown sugar
1 tablespoon vinegar or lemon juice
1 tablespoon instant minced onion
1 teaspoon mustard
4 to 5 drops liquid smoke, optional
2 to 3 lb. cut up fryer

Serves 4 to 6

Preheat oven to 350°.

Combine all ingredients except chicken in 2 cup measure.

Place chicken in 12×8-in. pan, cover with half the sauce. Bake, covered with foil, 45 minutes. Drain fat. Turn chicken, if desired, cover with remaining sauce. Bake uncovered 25 to 35 minutes, or until chicken is fork tender.

NOTE: Skin may be removed, if desired.

WAX PAPER

USE DISH

MICROWAVE AT HIGH.

MICROWAVE AT HIGH FOR HALF THE TIME.

Chicken Stew

This conventional recipe uses a broiler-fryer which makes it quick-cooking by conventional standards. If your recipe calls for a stewing chicken, substitute a broiler-fryer when adapting it for microwaving. While an older fowl can be microwaved at 50% (Medium), it takes almost as long to tenderize in the microwave as it would conventionally.

This recipe calls for oil to prevent sticking while the chicken browns. Since browning is not necessary, the oil can be omitted. We used a little to add flavor. Salt and liquid were reduced slightly because there is little evaporation during the short microwaving time.

Speedy Chicken Stew

REDUCE

6 tablespoons oil
2½ to 3½ lbs. broiler-fryer chicken pieces
6 tablespoons flour, divided
1 large onion, chopped
½ cup chopped celery
½ cup chopped green pepper

2¼ cups water, divided
2 teaspoons parsley flakes
1½ teaspoons salt
¼ teaspoon pepper
¼ teaspoon rosemary
1 teaspoon instant chicken bouillon granules

Serves 4 to 6

OMIT

Heat oil in Dutch oven or 5-qt. casserole over medium-high heat. Dredge chicken pieces in 4 tablespoons flour. Brown 4 to 5 pieces at a time in oil. Place on paper towels to drain. *OMIT*

Add vegetables to oil. Cook until softened, stirring occasionally. Stir in 2 cups water, seasonings and bouillon. Add chicken pieces. Cover and simmer over low heat 1 to 1¼ hours or until chicken is tender. Skim fat from broth if desired.

Combine ¼ cup water and 2 tablespoons flour. Stir into stew. Cook over medium-high heat 3 to 5 minutes, uncovered, or until mixture thickens, stirring frequently.

OMIT

REDUCE

MICROWAVE AT HIGH

MICROWAVE AT HIGH, REARRANGING AFTER HALF THE COOKING TIME.

BEFORE SERVING TIME.

MICROWAVE AT HIGH, STIRRING ONCE.

Converted Speedy Chicken Stew

1 or 2 tablespoons olive oil or butter, optional
1 large onion, chopped
½ cup chopped celery
½ cup chopped green pepper
2½ to 3½ lbs. broiler-fryer chicken pieces
6 tablespoons flour, divided
1¾ cups water, divided
2 teaspoons parsley flakes
1 teaspoon salt
¼ teaspoon pepper
¼ teaspoon rosemary
1 teaspoon instant chicken bouillon granules

Serves 4 to 6

Combine oil and vegetables in 5-qt. casserole. Cover. Microwave at High 4 to 5½ minutes, or until softened, stirring once.

Dredge chicken pieces in flour. Add to casserole and sprinkle with any flour remaining from dredging. Stir in 1½ cups water, seasonings and bouillon. Cover. Microwave at High 25 to 35 minutes, or until chicken is tender, rearranging after half the cooking time so least cooked portions are brought to outside of dish. Skim fat from broth, if desired.

Combine ¼ cup water and 2 tablespoons flour. Stir into stew. Microwave uncovered 3½ to 5½ minutes, or until mixture thickens, stirring before serving.

30 to 45 minutes at 50% (Medium)

2½ to 3 lb. chicken. 1½ to 2 cups water.

Casseroles: Raw Rice and Uncooked Chicken Pieces

Raw or converted long-grained rice needs time to rehydrate, so it takes almost as long to microwave as it does to cook conventionally. When it is used in a casserole, the total time may be too long for other ingredients. The preferred way to adapt a rice casserole is to substitute quick-cooking rice. (See page 52.)

If you wish to use raw or converted rice in a casserole, microwave it first until almost tender, then add the quicker-cooking meat. You may reduce liquid slightly, but you must have enough to rehydrate the rice.

Since this conventional recipe bakes for 1½ hours, we were able to use raw rice and still save time. With quick-cooking rice the casserole would be assembled at the beginning and microwaved at High just long enough to cook the chicken and rehydrate rice.

Chicken & Rice Casserole

1½ cups water ~REDUCE~
1 can (10¾-oz.) cream of
    mushroom soup
1 cup long-grain rice
½ cup chopped celery

½ cup chopped onion
1 envelope dry chicken
    noodle soup mix
2 to 3 lbs. broiler-fryer
    chicken pieces

OPTIONAL: MELTED BUTTER AND BOUQUET SAUCE FOR COLOR

Serves 4

OMIT

Preheat oven to 375°.   *PLASTIC WRAP*   *DISH*

Combine all ingredients except chicken in 12×8-in. baking pan. Arrange chicken pieces on top. Cover with foil, bake 1 hour.

Remove foil. Bake 30 to 40 minutes, or until chicken is tender and rice is cooked.

RESERVE CHICKEN   *ARRANGE CHICKEN OVER RICE. COVER WITH WAX PAPER. MICROWAVE AT HIGH, REARRANGING CHICKEN AFTER HALF THE TIME. LET STAND.*   *MICROWAVE AT HIGH THEN 50% (MEDIUM)*

Converted Chicken & Rice Casserole

1¼ cups water
1 can (10¾-oz.) cream of
    mushroom soup
1 cup long-grain rice
½ cup chopped celery
½ cup chopped onion
1 envelope dry chicken
    noodle soup mix
2 to 3 lbs. broiler-fryer
    chicken pieces
½ teaspoon melted butter
    mixed with ½ teaspoon
    bouquet sauce, optional

Serves 4

Combine water, soup, rice, celery, onion and dry soup mix in 12×8-in. baking dish. Cover tightly with plastic wrap. Microwave at High 5 minutes. Reduce power to 50% (Medium). Microwave 13 to 17 minutes, or until rice is almost tender.

Stir rice mixture. Arrange chicken pieces on top. Brush chicken pieces with butter and bouquet sauce mixture if desired. Cover with wax paper. Microwave at High 14 to 18 minutes, or until chicken is tender and rice is cooked, rearranging chicken after half the cooking time. Let stand 5 minutes.

22 to 32 minutes

2 to 3 lbs. chicken

How to Adapt Raw Rice Casseroles

Combine rice, liquid and seasonings in dish. Cover. Microwave at High and 50% (Medium) until rice is almost tender.

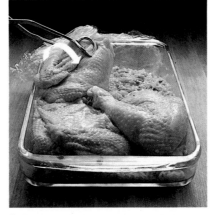

Stir rice. Add meat or quick-cooking ingredients. Microwave at High until meat is tender, stirring or rearranging once.

Casseroles: Cooked Chicken, Stirable

Be practical when adapting recipes for microwave. To reduce the liquid in this casserole, we simply omitted the milk rather than use only one part of a can of soup.

You may use High power if your casserole can be stirred during cooking, unless it contains a sensitive ingredient like cream. A crumb topping should be added after the final stirring.

OMIT OR USE 1 TABLESPOON FOR FLAVOR

OMIT   REDUCE

Baked Chicken Salad

2 tablespoons butter
   or margarine
1 cup diced celery
¼ cup chopped onion
2 cups cubed, cooked
   chicken
3 hard-cooked eggs, coarsely
   chopped
1 can (10¾-oz) cream of
   chicken soup

⅓ cup milk
¼ cup slivered almonds
1 tablespoon lemon juice
2 teaspoons chopped
   pimiento, optional
1 teaspoon salt
¼ teaspoon pepper
1 can (1½-oz.) shoestring
   potatoes, divided

Serves 4 to 6

OMIT

Preheat oven to 375°.   *OMIT*

In small skillet, melt butter and sauté celery and onion over medium-high heat until tender.

Combine all ingredients, except half of the shoestring potatoes in 1½-qt. casserole. Bake 45 to 55 minutes, or until heated through, topping with remaining potatoes during last 10 minutes.

1½ QT. CASSEROLE

MICROWAVE AT HIGH, STIR AND ADD TOPPING.

MICROWAVE AT HIGH COVERED.

Converted Baked Chicken Salad

3 eggs
1 cup diced celery
¼ cup chopped onion
2 cups cubed, cooked chicken
1 can (10¾-oz) cream of
   chicken soup, undiluted
¼ cup slivered almonds
1 tablespoon lemon juice
2 teaspoons chopped pimiento,
   optional
½ teaspoon salt
¼ teaspoon pepper
1 can (1½-oz.) shoestring
   potatoes, divided

Serves 4 to 6

Hard-cook eggs conventionally. Chop coarsely. Set aside.

Combine celery and onion in 1½-qt. casserole. Cover. Microwave at High 3 to 4 minutes, or until vegetables are tender. Stir in remaining ingredients, except half the shoestring potatoes. Microwave at High, uncovered, 3 minutes. Stir. Sprinkle with remaining potatoes. Microwave at High 2 to 3 minutes, or until heated through.

5 to 13 minutes

1½-qt. casserole. Varies with temperature of ingredients and amount of stirring.

Casseroles: Cooked Chicken, Non-stirable

Generally you should reduce the amount of liquid in a casserole by ¼ to ½, depending on the type of ingredients and the length of microwaving time; use your judgement. In this sample, we omitted the milk, but used the whole can of soup for convenience, and the full amount of mayonnaise for flavor, since both ingredients are very thick.

A layered casserole cannot be stirred, so we started it at High, then reduced the power to 50% (Medium) and rotated the dish halfway through cooking. Compare the difference between conventional and microwave cooking times.

Chicken & Vegetable Casserole

1 can (10¾-oz.) cream of
   chicken soup
½ cup mayonnaise or salad
   dressing
¼ cup milk *OMIT*
1 can (4-oz.) water chestnuts,
   chopped, optional
1½ teaspoons lemon juice
¾ teaspoon prepared
   mustard
¼ to ½ teaspoon curry
   powder
1 pkg. (10-oz.) frozen mixed
   vegetables, defrosted and
   drained   *MICROWAVE TO DEFROST*
2 cups cubed cooked
   chicken or turkey
⅔ cup shredded Cheddar
   cheese
¼ cup seasoned bread
   crumbs

Serves 4 to 6

OMIT

Preheat oven to 375°.

In medium mixing bowl combine soup, salad dressing, milk, water chestnuts, lemon juice and seasonings.

In 1½-qt. casserole, layer half the vegetables, half the chicken, half the sauce and half the cheese. Repeat layers. Top with bread crumbs. Bake 45 minutes to 1 hour or until heated through.

MICROWAVE AT HIGH, THEN 50% (MEDIUM) ROTATING DISH ¼ TURN AFTER HALF THE COOKING TIME.

Converted Chicken & Vegetable Casserole

1 can (10¾-oz.) cream of
   chicken soup
½ cup mayonnaise or salad
   dressing
1 can (4-oz.) water chestnuts,
   chopped, optional
1½ teaspoons lemon juice
¾ teaspoon prepared mustard
¼ to ½ teaspoon curry powder
1 pkg. (10-oz.) frozen mixed
   vegetables, defrosted in
   package at High 3 to 4
   minutes and drained
2 cups cubed cooked chicken
   or turkey
⅔ cup shredded Cheddar
   cheese
¼ cup seasoned bread
   crumbs

Serves 4 to 6

In medium bowl mix soup, salad dressing, water chestnuts, lemon juice and seasonings.

In 1½-qt. casserole, layer half each of vegetables, chicken, sauce and cheese. Repeat layers. Microwave at High 3 minutes. Reduce power to 50% (Medium). Microwave 10 to 12 minutes, or until heated through, rotating dish ¼ turn after half the cooking time. Top with bread crumbs.

High 3 to 5 minutes
50% (Medium) 9 to 18 minutes

1½-qt. casserole. Depending on temperature and amount of ingredients.

Fish & Shellfish

Converting Fish & Shellfish

Because of its speed and moisture retention, microwaving is an excellent way to prepare fish and shellfish. Before converting a conventional recipe, read the guidelines on pages 26 and 27.

Avoid overcooking these delicate foods. If your recipe contains long-cooking ingredients, add fish or shellfish toward the end of microwaving. We recommend 50% (Medium) power for microwaving shellfish in sauce. They can be microwaved at High power, but you should stir them often and check frequently to avoid overcooking.

When shellfish are cooked at High power, remove them from the oven while they are still slightly translucent at the center. Allow them to stand a few minutes to complete cooking.

Fish dumplings (quenelles) can be converted to microwaving without any change in ingredients. Bring water to boiling in a baking dish. Slip in the dumplings and microwave at 50% (Medium) power.

Fish mousse may be molded in cheesecloth or a souffle dish and placed in a dish of very hot water. Mousse is an airy mixture like a souffle, and must be microwaved at 30% (Medium-low) power.

How to Adapt Fish & Shellfish Recipes

Add fish or shellfish toward end of microwaving when recipe contains long-cooking ingredients.

Undercook shrimp slightly when using High power. They should be translucent inside. Let stand to finish cooking.

Use High power for fish fillets in a delicate sauce which can be stirred since microwaving time is very short.

Some Things That Don't Work and Why

Deep-fried Fish and Shrimp cannot be microwaved because the fat reaches dangerously high temperatures.

Pan-fried Fish and Breaded Shrimp should not be prepared in a browning dish because they may stick and break up.

Shellfish: Uncooked in Sturdy or Delicate Sauce

When recipes for uncooked shellfish are adapted for microwaving, the sauce should be cooked first and the shellfish added at the end to prevent overcooking. This rule also applies to gumbos and shellfish stews.

Sturdy sauces, like white sauce, can be microwaved first at High power. Delicate sauces containing cream or eggs and sauces which require simmering to develop flavor should be microwaved at 50% (Medium).

When shellfish is added to the hot sauce it begins to cook immediately. To avoid overcooking and toughening the shellfish, use 50% (Medium) power and allow standing time after microwaving.

In this conventional Shrimp Creole the shrimp are added at the end of cooking, so no change was needed in the recipe procedure. If your recipe directs you to add the shellfish at the beginning, remember to reserve them until the end of cooking when converting the recipe. Cooking time depends on the size as well as the amount of shellfish. Check for doneness frequently.

Shrimp Creole

3 tablespoons shortening	1½ teaspoons lemon juice
3 tablespoons flour	½ teaspoon pepper
¾ cup chopped onions	⅛ to ¼ teaspoon cayenne
½ cup chopped green onions	pepper, optional
½ cup chopped celery, with leaves	2 bay leaves
	½ teaspoon sugar
½ cup green pepper	½ teaspoon Worcestershire
1 large clove garlic, pressed	sauce
1 can (6-oz.) tomato paste	2 lbs. medium raw shrimp,
1 can (16-oz.) whole tomatoes	peeled and deveined
¾ cup water	
2 teaspoons salt	Serves 4 to 6

(handwritten notes: water → REDUCE; MICROWAVE AT HIGH)

In a large skillet melt shortening. Blend in flour and stir constantly until bubbly. Add onions, celery, green pepper and garlic. Sauté until onion is translucent. Stir in tomato paste until smooth. Add remaining ingredients except shrimp. Simmer over low heat, covered, for 1 hour stirring occasionally.

Add shrimp, cook over medium heat 10 to 15 minutes, or until shrimp are done. Do not overcook. Stir occasionally.

NOTE: This dish is best made in advance.

(handwritten notes: USE 2-QT. CASSEROLE; MICROWAVE AT 50% (MEDIUM); OMIT; MICROWAVE AT HIGH)

How to Adapt Shellfish

Prepare sturdy or delicate sauce, microwaving at High or 50% (Medium) as sauce requires.

Converted Shrimp Creole

    3 tablespoons shortening
    3 tablespoons flour
   ¾ cup chopped onions
   ½ cup chopped green onions
   ½ cup chopped celery, with
        leaves
   ½ cup green pepper
    1 large clove garlic, pressed
    1 can (6-oz.) tomato paste
    1 can (16-oz.) whole tomatoes
   ½ cup water
   ½ teaspoon salt
  1½ teaspoons lemon juice
   ½ teaspoon pepper
   ⅛ to ¼ teaspoon cayenne
        pepper, optional
    2 bay leaves
   ½ teaspoon sugar
   ½ teaspoon Worcestershire
        sauce
    2 lbs. medium raw shrimp,
        peeled and deveined

Serves 4 to 6

In 2-qt. casserole, melt shortening at High 1 to 2 minutes. Blend in flour. Add onions, celery, green pepper and garlic.

Microwave at High 3 to 4½ minutes, or until onion is translucent. Stir in tomato paste until smooth. Add remaining ingredients except shrimp. Cover. Microwave at 50% (Medium) 20 to 25 minutes, or until sauce is thick and bubbly, stirring once or twice.

Stir in shrimp. Cover. Microwave at 50% (Medium) 3½ to 7½ minutes, or until shrimp are opaque, stirring once or twice. Do not overcook. Let stand, covered, 3 to 5 minutes.

NOTE: This dish is best made in advance.

3 to 10 minutes

1 to 2 lb. medium shrimp and scallops. Depending on power, amount of shrimp, and amount of sauce, if used.

Add shellfish to hot sauce. Be sure to use 50% (Medium) power and microwave until shrimp are opaque, stirring once or twice.

Poached Fish

Conventionally, fish is poached in a liquid which seasons the fish, keeps it moist and helps it cook gently. In a microwave oven, fish can be poached without liquid, but when you are adapting a conventional recipe, use a small amount of liquid as a vehicle for seasonings. If wine is called for, it can be substituted for part of the water.

Many conventional recipes are finished with a sauce made from part of the poaching broth. For this type of recipe, add as much liquid as you will need to make the sauce. More time will be required to heat the liquid and poach the fish because of the increased volume. Traditionally, a whole fish is wrapped in cheesecloth to keep it moist on top and prevent it from breaking up when it is turned. This step is not needed in microwaving. A tight cover of plastic wrap holds in moisture. Be sure to turn back one edge of the wrap to make a small slot through which excess steam can escape. Otherwise, the wrap may split during microwaving.

How to Microwave Poached Whole Fish

Combine poaching ingredients in 12×8-in. baking dish. Cover with plastic wrap. Microwave at High 4 to 6 minutes.

Place fish in dish. Cover tightly with plastic wrap, turning back one edge to form a vent.

Microwave at High 8 to 11 minutes per lb. or until fish flakes easily with fork, rotating dish after half the cooking time.

Poaching Liquid

(handwritten: REDUCE)
(handwritten: 12 × 8 IN. DISH)

4 cups water
1 medium carrot, cut into
  ½-in. pieces
1 stalk celery, cut into
  1-in. pieces
1 small onion, sliced

3 slices lemon
2 peppercorns
1 bay leaf
1 teaspoon parsley flakes
1 teaspoon salt

(handwritten: OMIT)

Combine all ingredients in large skillet. Heat to boiling. Cover and simmer 8 to 10 minutes.

Whole Fish

(handwritten: MICROWAVE AT HIGH)

1 to 2 lb. fish (or block of fish, such as torsk), fresh or defrosted

Serves 4 to 8

(handwritten: OMIT)

Wrap whole fish in cheesecloth for ease in transferring fish after cooking. Place fish in liquid. Cover and simmer over medium heat 14 to 18 minutes or until fish flakes easily with fork, turning fish over after half the cooking time if liquid does not cover fish.

Fish Fillets

1 lb. fish fillets, fresh or defrosted

Serves 4 to 6

Arrange fish in liquid. Cover. Simmer over medium heat 5 to 7 minutes or until fish flakes easily with fork.

(handwritten: MICROWAVE AT HIGH REARRANGING AFTER HALF THE TIME)

(handwritten: ROTATE DISH)

Converted Poaching Liquid

¼ cup water
1 medium carrot, cut into
  ½-in. pieces
1 stalk celery, cut into
  1-in. pieces
1 small onion, sliced
3 slices lemon
2 peppercorns
1 bay leaf
1 teaspoon parsley flakes
¼ teaspoon salt

Microwave according to photo directions.

Whole Fish

1 to 2 lb. dressed fish (or block of fish) fresh or defrosted

Serves 4 to 8

Microwave according to photo directions.

6 to 15 minutes - 1 to 2 lb. fish

Depending on amount of fish and liquid.

Fish Fillets

1 lb. fish fillets, fresh or defrosted

Serves 4 to 8

Microwave according to photo directions.

5 to 10 minutes - 1 lb. fish

Depending on amount of liquid.

How to Microwave Poached Fish Fillets

Combine poaching ingredients in 12×8-in. baking dish. Cover with plastic wrap. Microwave at High 4 to 6 minutes.

Arrange fish in dish with thickest portions to outside. Overlap thin areas in center, if necessary. Cover with vented plastic wrap.

Microwave at High 5 to 7 minutes or until fish flakes easily with fork, rearranging fish after half the cooking time.

Fish Fillets: Sturdy Sauce

When adapting sauced fillets for microwaving, reduce the amount of liquid in the sauce, since it will not evaporate in the short cooking time. In this sample recipe, butter was not needed to keep the vegetables from sticking, but we used a little for flavor.

The sauce provided sufficient shielding for the fish, so we didn't use a cover because excess steam would make the sauce watery. We rotated the dish, rather than try to rearrange the fillets, which might break up. Fillets in a sturdy sauce, like tomatoes, can be micro-waved at High power. With a cream sauce, reduce the power to 50% (Medium) and double the time.

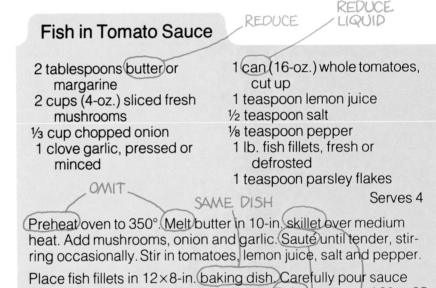

Fish in Tomato Sauce

REDUCE   *REDUCE LIQUID*

2 tablespoons (butter) or
    margarine
2 cups (4-oz.) sliced fresh
    mushrooms
⅓ cup chopped onion
1 clove garlic, pressed or
    minced

1 (can (16-oz.) whole tomatoes,
    cut up
1 teaspoon lemon juice
½ teaspoon salt
⅛ teaspoon pepper
1 lb. fish fillets, fresh or
    defrosted
1 teaspoon parsley flakes

Serves 4

OMIT   *SAME DISH*

(Preheat) oven to 350°. (Melt) butter in 10-in. skillet over medium heat. Add mushrooms, onion and garlic. (Sauté) until tender, stirring occasionally. Stir in tomatoes, lemon juice, salt and pepper.

Place fish fillets in 12×8-in. (baking dish.) Carefully pour sauce over fillets. Sprinkle with parsley flakes. Bake uncovered 30 to 35 minutes, or until fish flakes easily with fork.   *12×8 IN. DISH*

MICROWAVE AT HIGH, ROTATING DISH AFTER HALF THE COOKING TIME.   *MICROWAVE AT HIGH*

Converted Fish in Tomato Sauce

1 tablespoon butter or
    margarine
2 cups (4-oz.) sliced fresh
    mushrooms
⅓ cup chopped onion
1 clove garlic, pressed or
    minced

1 can (16-oz.) whole tomatoes,
    cut up, discard ¼ cup liquid
1 teaspoon lemon juice
½ teaspoon salt
⅛ teaspoon pepper
1 lb. fish fillets, fresh or
    defrosted
1 teaspoon parsley flakes

Serves 4

Place butter, mushrooms, onion and garlic in 12×8-in. baking dish. Microwave at High 3½ to 5½ minutes, or until vegetables are tender, stirring after half the cooking time. Stir in tomatoes, lemon juice, salt and pepper. Push sauce to side of dish.

Arrange fillets in dish with thickest portions to outside. Carefully cover fillets with sauce. Sprinkle with parsley flakes. Microwave at High 5½ to 8 minutes, or until fish flakes easily with fork, rotating dish after half the cooking time.

5 to 12 minutes, 1 lb. fish

Depending on amount of sauce

Fish Fillets: Delicate Sauce

When a delicate sauce made with cheese or cream is stabilized with flour and can be stirred, you may use High power for the short time needed to microwave fish fillets. If your fish is baked in cream without the addition of flour, reduce the power to 50% (Medium) and double the microwaving time.

In the microwave version of this recipe, the sauce is made in the same dish which will be used to cook the fish. After half the cooking time, the fillets are rearranged and re-covered with sauce. This serves the same purpose as stirring. The sauce is stirred again before serving.

Fish in Cheese Sauce

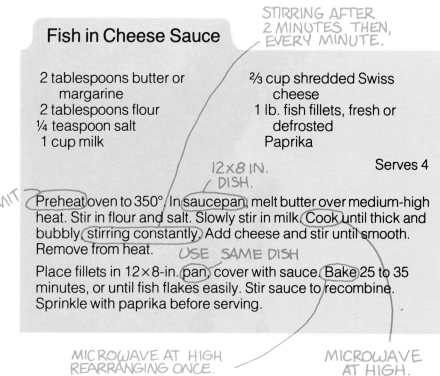

2 tablespoons butter or
  margarine
2 tablespoons flour
¼ teaspoon salt
1 cup milk

⅔ cup shredded Swiss
  cheese
1 lb. fish fillets, fresh or
  defrosted
Paprika

Serves 4

STIRRING AFTER 2 MINUTES THEN, EVERY MINUTE.

12×8 IN. DISH.

OMIT

Preheat oven to 350°. In saucepan, melt butter over medium-high heat. Stir in flour and salt. Slowly stir in milk. Cook until thick and bubbly, stirring constantly. Add cheese and stir until smooth. Remove from heat.

USE SAME DISH

Place fillets in 12×8-in. pan, cover with sauce. Bake 25 to 35 minutes, or until fish flakes easily. Stir sauce to recombine. Sprinkle with paprika before serving.

MICROWAVE AT HIGH REARRANGING ONCE.

MICROWAVE AT HIGH.

Converted Fish in Cheese Sauce

2 tablespoons butter or
  margarine
2 tablespoons flour
¼ teaspoon salt
1 cup milk
⅔ cup shredded Swiss cheese
1 lb. fish fillets, fresh or
  defrosted
Paprika

Serves 4

In 12×8-in. dish, melt butter at High 20 to 45 seconds. Stir in flour and salt. Blend in milk. Microwave at High 5 to 8 minutes, or until thickened, stirring after 2 minutes and then every other minute. Add cheese, stirring until melted.

Place fillets in dish. Spoon sauce to cover fish. Microwave at High 10 to 14 minutes, or until fish flakes easily, rearranging and covering with sauce after half the cooking time. Stir sauce to recombine. Sprinkle with paprika.

9 to 16 minutes
1 lb. fish

Depending on amount of sauce.

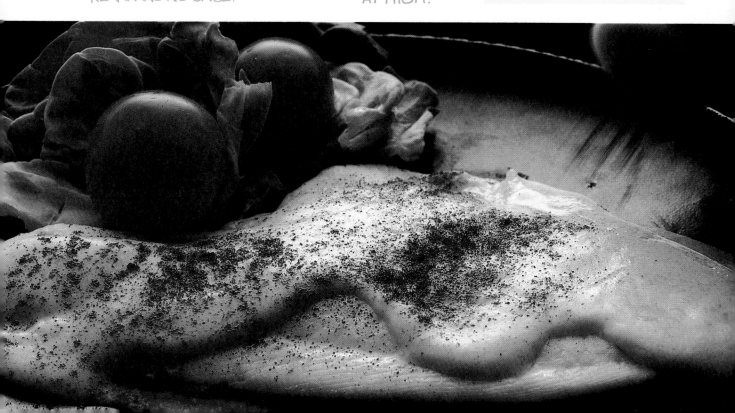

Loaves: Canned or Cooked Fish (or Meat)

Use these guidelines to adapt loaves made with salmon, tuna or ham. Since these ingredients do not give off fat or juices during cooking, the proportion of filler (crumbs), liquid and eggs remains the same as your conventional recipe. The only changes needed are the microwave method and time.

If you are using these guidelines to adapt a ham loaf which contains uncooked ground pork, microwave the loaf at High 5 minutes. Reduce power to 50% (Medium) and microwave to an internal temperature of 160°, about 23 to 28 minutes for a 1½-lb. loaf.

Salmon Loaf

1 can (16-oz.) salmon, drained and liquid combined with enough milk to make ½ cup
2 eggs
½ cup dry bread crumbs
½ cup chopped onion
1 tablespoon parsley flakes
1 teaspoon grated lemon peel
½ teaspoon salt
⅛ teaspoon pepper

Serves 4

OMIT — Preheat oven to 350°. In *(LOAF DISH)* mixing bowl, flake salmon, removing bones and skin. With a fork, beat in eggs; mix in remaining ingredients. Spread in well greased 8×4-in. loaf pan or form into loaf shape in 8-in. square baking pan. Bake, uncovered, 50 to 60 minutes or until center is firm and loaf is golden brown. Loosen edges and turn out of loaf pan; serve in slices. For square pan, cut into squares and remove from pan.

NOT SUITABLE — *OMIT* — *MICROWAVE AT 50% (MEDIUM)* — *SAME DISH* — *WILL NOT BROWN*

Converted Salmon Loaf

1 can (16-oz.) salmon, drained and liquid combined with enough milk to make ½ cup
2 eggs
½ cup dry bread crumbs
½ cup chopped onion
1 tablespoon parsley flakes
1 teaspoon grated lemon peel
½ teaspoon salt
⅛ teaspoon pepper

Serves 4

In loaf dish, flake salmon, removing bones and skin. Blend in remaining ingredients. Press out evenly in dish. Microwave at 50% (Medium) 18 to 24 minutes, or until center is firm, rotating once or twice. Loosen edges and turn out of dish. Serve in slices.

15 to 30 minutes

Depending on liquid and filler.

Casseroles: Canned or Cooked Fish in Sauce

The general guideline for adapting fish casseroles is to reduce the amount of liquid by ¼ to ⅓, but this is not an unbreakable rule. Be flexible and practical. In this sample recipe we omitted the milk, but used the full amount of canned soup and evaporated milk. This is less than a ¼ reduction, but since the casserole is meant to be creamy, the extra liquid made very little difference and we didn't have leftover soup and milk to refrigerate.

When your casserole can be stirred, use High power. If cream were substituted for evaporated milk in this recipe, you could still use High power by stirring more frequently.

Microwave a layered casserole at 50% (Medium) and rotate the dish after half the cooking time. A layered casserole assembled with sturdy, room temperature ingredients, such as canned fish, cooked vegetables and tomato sauce, can be microwaved at High with a single rotation because of the very short heating time.

Tuna Casserole

1 pkg. (7-oz.) elbow macaroni, cooked and drained
3 hard-cooked eggs, chopped
1 can (9¼-oz.) tuna, drained
1 can (10¾-oz.) cream of chicken soup

1 can (5.3-oz.) evaporated milk (¾ cup)
¼ cup milk — OMIT
¼ cup chopped onion
1 tablespoon parsley flakes
1 teaspoon salt — REDUCE
¼ teaspoon pepper

Serves 6 to 8

OMIT — Preheat oven to 375°.

Combine all ingredients in 2-qt. casserole. Bake 40 to 50 minutes, or until hot. Garnish with sliced hard-cooked egg, if desired.

MICROWAVE AT HIGH, STIRRING ONCE OR TWICE.

Converted Tuna Casserole

3 eggs
1 pkg. (7-oz.) elbow macaroni, cooked and drained
1 can (9¼-oz.) tuna, drained
1 can (10¾-oz.) cream of chicken soup
1 can (5.3-oz.) evaporated milk (¾ cup)
¼ cup chopped onion
1 tablespoon parsley flakes
½ teaspoon salt
⅛ teaspoon pepper

Serves 6 to 8

Hard-cook eggs conventionally. Peel and chop.

Combine all ingredients in 2-qt. casserole. Microwave at High 7 to 11 minutes, or until heated through, stirring once or twice. Garnish with sliced hard-cooked egg, if desired.

6 to 13 minutes

Depending on liquid and amount of other ingredients.

Eggs & Cheese

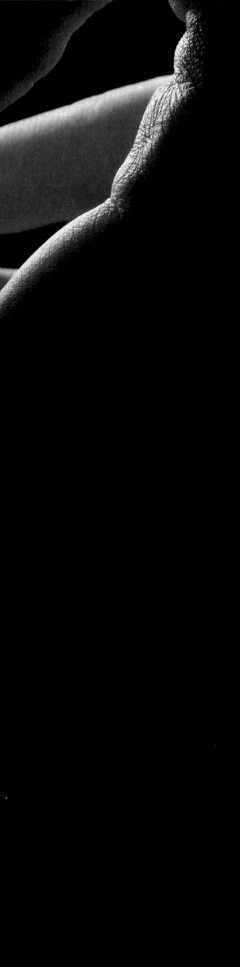

Converting Eggs

The heating patterns of individual ovens affects the way eggs cook. Two ovens of the same make and model may not produce the same results. If your oven has a very uneven pattern, you may have difficulty with poached or shirred eggs and omelet mixtures.

Size of eggs influences the volume and moisture content of foods. Unless otherwise specified, most conventional recipes use large eggs. If your eggs are a different size, it will affect the total microwaving time and the consistency of the result.

Microwave-scrambled eggs are superior to conventionally cooked and can be prepared in any oven. Since the eggs are stirred, they can be microwaved at High power. Standing time is essential to any egg dish. It completes cooking without toughening delicate eggs. Use 50% (Medium) power for poached and shirred eggs, or eggs baked in a nest of vegetables or hash. Rotate the dish when microwaving several eggs at once.

Egg Foo Yung can be microwaved in a browning dish. French omelets made in a browning dish are not satisfactory, but omelet mixtures can be microwaved in a pie plate, then filled and folded in the usual way. The bottom will not be brown and the texture will be somewhat different from a conventional omelet.

Converting Cheese

Microwave cooks make great use of cheese to dress up sandwiches and simple main dishes. Cheese-topped casseroles are similar to coventionally baked, but the cheese should be added at the end of microwaving because it melts rapidly and toughens easily.

Processed and softer cheeses are easier to use than hard, natural cheeses. When cheese is included in a dish which must be heated for some time, select 50% (Medium) power. At High power the cheese mixture must be stirred frequently.

Some Things That Don't Work and Why

Hard-cooked Eggs in the shell must never be made in a microwave oven. They will burst.

Whole Hard-cooked Eggs should not be reheated by microwave. Slice or chop them first. Even when shelled they can burst.

French Omelets cannot be made in a browning dish.

Cheese Strata in a dish over 1½-in. deep does not cook evenly.

Omelets

Microwaved omelets do not crust and brown because they are not made on a hot surface. With the exception of Eggs Foo Yung, the browning dish is not satisfactory for omelets. Use a 9-in. pie plate.

Puffy Omelets adapt easily. They are similar to conventionally cooked, but are faster and easier to make because you don't need to heat both the range top and the oven.

Whether you are preparing a Puffy Omelet, a French Omelet or an Italian Fritata, the technique for microwaved omelets is the same. Use 50% (Medium) power to set the delicate eggs without overcooking. When the eggs are partially set, lift the edges with a spatula to allow the uncooked portions to spread out evenly. Do this several times when microwaving French or Italian omelets which are more liquid because the egg whites are not beaten separately.

Notice that the test for doneness is slightly different for a microwaved omelet. The center should be almost set. It will complete cooking in the short time needed to serve it.

Puffy Omelet

4 eggs, separated	⅛ teaspoon pepper
¼ cup milk	1 tablespoon butter or
½ teaspoon salt	margarine
¼ teaspoon baking powder	Filling

Serves 2 to 4

Preheat ~~oven~~ to 325°. *OMIT*

In medium mixing bowl, beat egg whites until stiff, but not dry. Set aside. Combine remaining ingredients, except butter and filling in small bowl. Fold yolk mixture into egg whites with rubber spatula. Set aside. *USE 9 IN. PIE PLATE*

Over medium heat, melt butter in 10-in. skillet with heat proof handle. Add egg mixture. Reduce heat to low and cook 8 to 10 minutes, or until light brown on bottom. Bake in oven 8 to 11 minutes, or until knife inserted in center comes out clean.

Sprinkle filling over half of omelet. Loosen omelet with spatula and fold in half. Gently slide onto serving plate.

PARTIALLY SET, LIFT EDGES.　　*CENTER IS ALMOST SET.*　　*MICROWAVE AT 50% (MEDIUM)*

MICROWAVE AT HIGH.

Microwave Tips for Four

Eggs Foo Yung. Preheat browning dish. Add butter. Fold vegetables into well beaten eggs. Microwave at 50% (Medium) until eggs are almost set.

Converted Puffy Omelet

 4 eggs, separated
¼ cup milk
½ teaspoon salt
¼ teaspoon baking powder
⅛ teaspoon pepper
 1 tablespoon butter or
    margarine
    Filling

Serves 2 to 4

In medium mixing bowl, beat egg whites until stiff, but not dry. Set aside. Combine remaining ingredients, except butter and filling in small bowl. Fold yolk mixture into egg whites with rubber spatula. Set aside.

In 9-in. pie plate, microwave butter at High 30 to 45 seconds, or until melted. Pour eggs into plate. Microwave at 50% (Medium) 3 to 5 minutes, or until partially set. Lift edges of omelet to allow uncooked portion to spread evenly over dish. Microwave 2½ to 4½ minutes, or until center is almost set. Sprinkle filling over half of omelet. Loosen omelet with spatula and fold in half. Gently slide onto serving plate.

4½ to 11 minutes

Puffy 4 egg omelet

Types of Omelets

Puffy Omelet. Fold egg yolk mixture into stiffly beaten whites. Microwave in pie plate as directed, lifting edges of omelet once during microwaving.

French Omelet. Pour lightly beaten eggs into butter in pie plate. Microwave at 50% (Medium), lifting edges with spatula several times. Fill and roll or fold.

Italian Fritata. Microwave vegetables with small amount of olive oil until tender-crisp. Mix into lightly beaten eggs. Microwave in pie plate at 50% (Medium) lifting edges several times.

Fondue & Rarebit

Cheeses vary in hardness and fat or moisture content. Length of aging, duration and type of storage in both store and home, all affect the way cheese melts. Softer cheeses are easier to melt and incorporate with the liquid in a fondue or rarebit. Heat the liquid first, then use 50% (Medium) power after the cheese is stirred in.

For this recipe we got excellent results using a very fresh natural Swiss cheese. If the cheese available in your store seems firm, substitute process cheese or Gruyere, or increase stirring to once every minute. A wire whisk is the best tool for stirring fondue or rarebit.

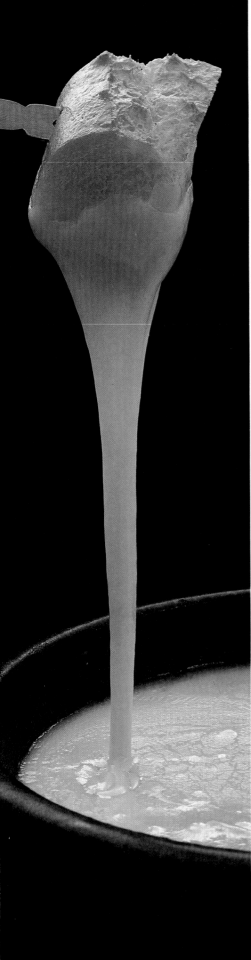

Swiss Fondue

REDUCE

USE 2 QT. CASSEROLE

1 clove garlic, cut into halves	⅛ teaspoon nutmeg
1½ cups white wine	Dash pepper
4 cups (1-lb.) shredded natural Swiss or Gruyere cheese	1 tablespoon brandy French bread, cut into 1-in. cubes
3 tablespoons flour	

Serves 4

Rub cut clove of garlic on bottom and side of heavy skillet or fondue dish. Add wine. Heat over low heat until bubbles rise to surface (do not boil). *MICROWAVE AT 50% (MEDIUM)*

Combine cheese, flour, nutmeg and pepper. Add cheese mixture about ½ cup at a time to wine, stirring constantly over low heat until cheese is melted. Stir in brandy. Keep warm over low heat. Serve with bread cubes for dipping.

ADD ALL AT ONCE.   *EVERY OTHER MINUTE*   *NOT NEEDED*

Converted Swiss Fondue

1 clove garlic, cut into halves	⅛ teaspoon nutmeg
1 cup white wine	Dash pepper
4 cups (1-lb.) shredded natural Swiss or Gruyere cheese	1 tablespoon brandy French bread, cut into 1-in. cubes
3 tablespoons flour	

Serves 4

Rub a 2-qt. casserole with cut garlic. Add wine. Microwave at 50% (Medium) 3 to 4 minutes or until bubbles form (do not boil).

Combine cheese, flour, nutmeg and pepper. Add to wine. Microwave 4½ to 6½ minutes or until cheese is melted, stirring every other minute. Stir in brandy. Reheat if necessary.

Serve with bread cubes for dipping.

3½ to 8 minutes

1 lb. shredded cheese,
1 cup liquid

Casseroles: Cheese Sauce

Cheese sauce is based on white sauce. Since these sauces microwave for such a short time, cook the flour and butter briefly before adding liquid to avoid the pasty flavor of raw flour.

Although cheese is a delicate food, it can be microwaved at High power when it is stirred into a hot sauce. If your conventional recipe calls for diced cheese, substitute shredded cheese. Chunks of cheese would attract too much microwave energy and require excessive stirring.

For this recipe, we reduced the amount of sauce by ¼, because it would not evaporate during the short microwaving time. Since all the ingredients were hot, we sprinkled the crumbs on top and rotated the dish once. If your casserole contains refrigerated ingredients, such as leftover meat, vegetables, rice or pasta, reserve the topping. Increase the time slightly and stir the casserole once or twice during heating. Then sprinkle on the topping and heat briefly.

Macaroni & Cheese

MICROWAVE AT HIGH, ROTATING DISH AFTER HALF THE COOKING TIME.

¼ cup dry bread crumbs
5 tablespoons butter or
   margarine, divided
¼ cup finely chopped onion
¼ cup flour
½ teaspoon salt   *REDUCE*

⅛ teaspoon pepper
2 cups milk
2 cups (8-oz.) shredded
   Cheddar cheese
1 pkg. (7-oz.) elbow macaroni,
   cooked and drained

Serves 6

OMIT ~~Preheat~~ oven to 350°. Combine bread crumbs and 1 tablespoon melted butter. Set aside.   *2 QT. CASSEROLE*

In saucepan, saute onion in 4 tablespoons butter over medium heat until tender. Blend in flour and seasonings. Slowly stir in milk. Cook until thick and bubbly, stirring constantly.

Mix in cheese until melted. Add macaroni. Pour mixture into 1½-qt. casserole. Sprinkle with bread crumb mixture. Bake 30 to 35 minutes or until heated through.

MICROWAVE AT HIGH STIRRING EVERY MINUTE.

MICROWAVE TO COOK.

Converted Macaroni & Cheese

¼ cup dry bread crumbs
4 tablespoons butter or
   margarine, divided
¼ cup finely chopped onion
3 tablespoons flour
½ teaspoon salt

⅛ teaspoon pepper
1½ cups milk
2 cups (8-oz.) grated Cheddar
   cheese
1 pkg. (7-oz.) elbow macaroni,
   cooked and drained

Serves 6

Combine bread crumbs and 1 tablespoon melted butter. Set aside. In 2-qt. casserole, combine onion and 3 tablespoons butter. Microwave at High 1½ to 2½ minutes or until onion is tender.

Stir in flour and seasonings until smooth. Microwave 30 to 45 seconds or until bubbly. Blend in milk smoothly. Microwave 4½ to 6 minutes or until thickened, stirring every minute.

Stir in cheese until melted. Microwave 15 to 20 seconds if needed. Mix in macaroni. Sprinkle with bread crumb mixture. Microwave 4½ to 6 minutes or until heated through, rotating dish after half the time.

4 to 10 minutes

2-qt. casserole

Souffles

Microwaved souffles do not brown and crust on the outside, but this is actually an advantage. When a souffle is baked conventionally, opening the oven door exposes it to cold air. The sudden change in temperature shrinks the crust and collapses the souffle. In microwaving, heat is in the food, not the air, so the souffle does not fall as easily. You may even slam the oven door without damaging the souffle.

Souffles must be microwaved at a lower power setting, such as 30% (Medium-Low), since they are very airy mixtures of delicate cream, cheese and beaten eggs. Expect some unevenness during rising. This should level out as the souffle cooks. If you see that one side is rising faster than another, rotate the dish so that the high spot is in the area of the oven where the low side was. If the outer edges of the souffle are overcooking, shield them with a ring of foil during the last ⅓ of the microwaving time.

Herbed Cheese Souffle

¼ cup butter or margarine
¼ cup flour
1 teaspoon salt
   Dash cayenne pepper
1½ cups light cream or
   evaporated milk

1 cup shredded Cheddar
   cheese
6 eggs separated
1 tablespoon parsley flakes
½ teaspoon thyme leaves
1 teaspoon cream of tartar

Serves 6 to 8

OMIT

1½ QT.
CASSEROLE

MICROWAVE
AT HIGH

(Preheat) oven to 325°.

Melt butter in medium saucepan over medium heat. Blend in flour, salt and pepper. Slowly stir in cream. Cook, stirring occasionally, until sauce is thick and smooth. Add cheese, stirring constantly until melted. Remove from heat.

In small bowl, beat egg yolks lightly. Blend in a small amount of the hot sauce. Pour egg yolk mixture into remaining sauce, stirring quickly to avoid lumping. Mix in parsley and thyme. Set aside.

In 2-qt. mixing bowl at highest speed of electric mixer, beat egg whites and cream of tartar until stiff peaks form. Gently fold cheese mixture into egg whites. Pour mixture into 2-qt. souffle dish. (Bake) 1 hour, or until puffy and brown.

MICROWAVE AT
30% (MEDIUM-LOW), ROTATING
DISH 3 OR 4 TIMES.

MICROWAVE AT
HIGH, STIRRING
AFTER 2 MINUTES,
THEN EVERY MINUTE.

How to Microwave Souffle

Microwave at 30% (Medium-Low). Souffle may rise higher on one side.

Converted Herbed Cheese Souffle

¼ cup butter or margarine
¼ cup flour
1 teaspoon salt
  Dash cayenne pepper
1½ cups light cream or
    evaporated milk
1 cup shredded Cheddar
  cheese
6 eggs separated
1 tablespoon parsley flakes
½ teaspoon thyme leaves
1 teaspoon cream of tartar

Serves 6 to 8

In 1½-qt. casserole, microwave butter at High 45 seconds to 1¼ minutes, or until melted. Blend in flour, salt and pepper. With wire whip, stir in cream. Microwave at High 3½ to 6½ minutes, or until sauce is thick and smooth, stirring after 2 minutes and then every minute. Stir in cheese until melted.

In small bowl, beat egg yolks lightly. Blend in a small amount of the hot sauce. Pour the egg yolk mixture into remaining sauce, stirring quickly to avoid lumping. Add parsley and thyme. Set aside.

In 2-qt. mixing bowl at highest speed of electric mixer, beat egg whites and cream of tartar until stiff peaks form. Gently fold cheese mixture into egg whites.

Pour mixture into 2-qt. souffle dish. Microwave at 30% (Medium-Low) 25 to 35 minutes, or until top is dry, rotating dish 3 or 4 times as needed.

20 to 37 minutes

6 eggs

Rotate dish so that high side is in the position occupied by the lowest area.

Souffle evens out during microwaving. Number of rotations needed depends on the oven's cooking pattern.

Quiche

Microwaved quiches are excellent, but several changes are needed when converting a conventional recipe. The conventional quiche is a custard mixture which is poured into an uncooked pie shell and then baked. For a microwaved quiche, the pie shell is microwaved first, so it can crisp and dry. An unbaked shell would absorb moisture from the filling and be soggy.

When converting the custard mixture, reduce the amount of liquid slightly. While you may use either evaporated milk or half & half, evaporated milk is more stable. If your oven has an uneven heating pattern, half & half may curdle.

Partial cooking of the custard mixture before it is poured into the baked shell allows you to stir it as it thickens and results in a smoother filling. Since eggs and cream are delicate foods, use 50% (Medium) power.

After the filling is poured into the shell, rotate the quiche ¼ turn after each ¼ of cooking time. This helps the custard set evenly.

Quiche Lorraine

9-in. unbaked pie or quiche shell, below	4 eggs
12 slices bacon	2 cups half & half
1 cup shredded natural Swiss or Gruyere cheese	¾ teaspoon salt
	⅛ teaspoon pepper
	Dash nutmeg

Serves 6

Prepare pie shell. Preheat oven to 425°.

In medium skillet over medium heat, fry bacon until crisp. Drain on paper towels. Crumble.

Sprinkle bacon and cheese in pie shell. In medium bowl, beat eggs with remaining ingredients. Pour into crust.

Bake uncovered 15 minutes. Reduce oven temperature to 325°. Bake 35 to 40 minutes, or until knife inserted halfway between center and edge comes out clean. Let stand 10 minutes before cutting.

Handwritten annotations:
- BAKED
- RACK OR PAPER TOWELS
- MICROWAVE AT 50% (MEDIUM) TO HEAT, STIRRING EVERY OTHER MINUTE.
- MICROWAVE AT 50% (MEDIUM) ROTATING DISH ¼ TURN EVERY ¼ OF COOKING TIME.
- 1 TABLESPOON BUTTER FOR COLOR
- REDUCE; USE EVAPORATED MILK, OPTIONAL.
- AND BAKE
- OMIT
- MICROWAVE AT HIGH.
- QT. CASSEROLE

Pie or Quiche Shell

⅓ cup plus 1 tablespoon shortening	½ teaspoon salt
1 cup flour	2 to 3 tablespoons cold water

Makes one 9-in. crust

In medium bowl, cut shortening into flour and salt until particles are size of small peas. Sprinkle in water, 1 tablespoon at a time, tossing with a fork until all flour is moistened and pastry almost cleans side of bowl.

Gather into a ball. Flatten to ½-in. round. Roll out on floured board to a circle 2-in. larger than inverted 9-in. pie plate or quiche dish.

Fit loosely into dish. Trim overhang to ½-in. Fold edge to form standing rim and flute. MICROWAVE BEFORE FILLING.

Handwritten annotations:
- COMBINED WITH 3 DROPS FOOD COLORING OPTIONAL.
- MIXTURE

How to Microwave Quiche

Microwave pastry shell and partially cook custard before assembling quiche.

Rotate dish ¼ turn after each ¼ of cooking time.

Converted Quiche Lorraine

9-in. baked pie shell, below	1 can (13-oz.) evaporated milk
12 slices bacon	or 1¾ cups half & half
1 cup shredded natural Swiss	¾ teaspoon salt
or Gruyere cheese	⅛ teaspoon pepper
4 eggs	Dash nutmeg

Serves 6

Prepare shell. Place 6 strips of bacon on 3 layers of paper towel; cover with paper towel. Place remaining strips on top. Cover with paper towel. Microwave at High 9 to 12 minutes, or until bacon looks slightly underdone. Let stand 3 to 5 minutes to brown and crisp.

Crumble bacon. Sprinkle bacon and cheese in pie or quiche shell. In 1-qt. casserole, beat eggs with remaining ingredients. Microwave at 50% (Medium) 5 to 8 minutes, or until thoroughly heated, stirring every other minute. Stir and pour into shell.

Microwave 13 to 21 minutes, or until knife inserted halfway between center and edge comes out clean and quiche seems set, rotating dish ¼ turn after each ¼ cooking time. Let stand 10 minutes before cutting.

Pie Shell

⅓ cup shortening	2 to 3 tablespoons cold water
1 to 2 tablespoons butter or	combined with 3 drops
margarine	yellow food coloring,
1 cup flour	optional
½ teaspoon salt	

Makes one 9-in. crust

Prepare crust as directed in conventional recipe.

Prick crust with fork at ⅛-in. intervals at bend of dish and ½-in. apart on bottom and sides of dish. Microwave at High 4½ to 6½ minutes, or until crust is dry and bottom is opaque; rotate dish after half the time.

Soups

Converting Soups

The guidelines for adapting soups for microwaving depend on the type of soup. Clear and brothy soups made with vegetables, tender chicken or prepared soup stock may be microwaved at High power. Use 50% (Medium) power to microwave soups containing less tender meats. Reduce the amount of liquid by ¼ and cut meat and vegetables in small pieces.

Chowders and cream soups made with milk can also be microwaved at High power. Select a container which will hold twice the volume of soup, because milk boils higher in a microwave oven than it does conventionally.

Use High power and less liquid to precook vegetables for pureed soups. Very dense purees, and delicate ones combined with cream and eggs, should be heated at 50% (Medium) power.

Soup made with dried beans or peas require the full amount of liquid. Dried vegetables need water to rehydrate; water will evaporate due to long microwaving time.

How to Microwave Soup Stock

Combine soup bones, water and seasonings in large casserole. Cover. Microwave at High until water boils.

Reduce power to 50% (Medium). Microwave until meat is soft, stirring and skimming once or twice, if necessary.

Scrape meat and marrow from bones. Cut in small pieces. Return meat, marrow and bones to pot, microwave until meat is tender.

How to Adapt Beef-Vegetable Soup

Cut beef and potatoes in ½-in. cubes. Slice other vegetables thinly. Small, uniform pieces cook more evenly.

Microwave beef in 1 cup of water, covered, at 50% (Medium) for 20 minutes.

Reduce amount of water added with vegetables. Microwave until meat and vegetables are tender.

Soups: Broth

Soup stock is usually made with less tender cuts of meat or poultry, which require a lower power setting to tenderize. If you are making chicken soup with a broiler-fryer, you may shorten cooking time by microwaving both chicken and vegetables at High power.

In this sample recipe, the beef is cooked until tender before the vegetables and remaining water are added. For the microwave version, we cooked the meat only partially. It tenderized in the time needed to microwave the vegetables at 50% (Medium) power. Notice that the vege-

tables are cut in small pieces for uniform cooking.

We used the same quantity of water to cook the beef, but reduced the amount added with the vegetables because it would not evaporate during micro-waving. Yield of both soups is the same.

Beef-Vegetable Soup

1 tablespoon oil *OMIT*
1 lb. beef boneless chuck or
   round, cut into ½-in.
   cubes
5 cups water, divided *REDUCE*
1 tablespoon instant beef
   bouillon granules
1 teaspoon salt
¼ teaspoon marjoram
   leaves
3 peppercorns or ⅛
   teaspoon pepper

1 bay leaf
1 whole allspice
1 can (16-oz.) whole
   tomatoes, cut up (with
   liquid)
3 medium carrots, cut into
   ½-in. slices *¼-IN. SLICES*
2 medium potatoes, cut into
   ¾-in. cubes *½-IN. CUBES*
1 stalk celery, cut into ½-in.
   slices *THIN SLICES*
1 small onion, sliced

Makes 2 quarts

OMIT Heat oil over medium heat in Dutch oven. Add beef and cook until brown, stirring occasionally. *3-QT. CASSEROLE*

Stir in 1 cup water, bouillon granules and seasonings. Cover; simmer over low heat 1¼ to 1½ hours, or until beef is tender.

Add remaining water and vegetables. Heat to boiling. Cover; simmer over low heat 40 to 50 minutes, or until vegetables are tender. *OMIT*

MICROWAVE AT HIGH, THEN 50% (MEDIUM)

MICROWAVE AT 50% (MEDIUM)

Converted Beef-Vegetable Soup

1 lb. boneless beef chuck or
   round, cut into ½-in. cubes
4 cups water, divided
1 tablespoon instant beef
   bouillon granules
1 teaspoon salt
¼ teaspoon marjoram leaves
3 peppercorns or ⅛ teaspoon
   pepper
1 bay leaf
1 whole allspice
1 can (16-oz.) whole tomatoes,
   cut up (with liquid)
3 medium carrots, thinly sliced
2 medium potatoes, cut into
   ½-in. cubes
1 stalk celery, cut into ¼-in.
   slices
1 small onion, sliced

Makes 2 quarts

Combine beef, 1 cup water, bouillon granules and seasonings in 3-qt. casserole. Cover. Microwave at High 5 minutes. Reduce power to 50% (Medium). Microwave 20 minutes.

Stir in remaining water and vegetables. Re-cover. Microwave 45 to 55 minutes, or until vegetables are tender. Let stand 10 minutes.

10 minutes to 1¼ hours

Depending on ingredients. Meatless soups require the shorter times.

Soups: Cream

Microwaving enhances the flavor of vegetables and retains their nutrients. Your microwaved soups should be more full bodied and fresh tasting than the conventional versions.

Most vegetables contain natural moisture and very little water is needed to microwave them. Compare the conventional recipe with the microwave adaptation. It is important to reduce salt, too.

If your soup is pureéd, you may want to thin it with a little more water or broth after cooking. In this conventional example, the soup is thickened with flour and cooked over medium heat. This prevents scorching the milk and reduces the soup. We tried using the same amount of flour in the microwave soup, but found it needed more thickening. If your recipe calls for cream rather than milk, you can microwave it at High power, but will need to stir it more frequently.

Cream of Potato Soup

INCREASE

3 cups diced potatoes
2 stalks celery, sliced
1 small onion, chopped
1 cup water → REDUCE
1 teaspoon salt
1 teaspoon parsley flakes

⅛ teaspoon pepper
1 teaspoon instant chicken bouillon granules
2 cups milk, divided
3 tablespoons flour
3 tablespoons butter or margarine

Makes 1 quart

CASSEROLE   OMIT

Combine potatoes, celery, onion, water, seasonings and bouillon granules in 2-qt. saucepan. Bring to boil. Cover and cook over medium heat 13 to 16 minutes, or until potatoes are tender.

Combine ¼ cup milk with flour until smooth. Add flour mixture, remaining milk and butter to potato mixture. Cook over medium heat until mixture boils, stirring constantly.

THICKENED   SEVERAL   MICROWAVE   MICROWAVE AT
             TIMES   AT HIGH   HIGH, STIRRING ONCE.

Converted Cream of Potato Soup

3 cups diced potatoes
2 stalks celery, sliced
1 small onion, chopped
¼ cup water
½ teaspoon salt
1 teaspoon parsley flakes
⅛ teaspoon pepper
1 teaspoon instant chicken bouillon granules
2 cups milk, divided
4 tablespoons flour
3 tablespoons butter or margarine

Makes 1 quart

Combine potatoes, celery, onion, water, seasonings and bouillon granules in 2-qt. casserole. Cover. Microwave at High 7 to 10 minutes, or until vegetables are tender, stirring after half the cooking time.

Combine ¼ cup milk with flour until smooth. Stir flour mixture, remaining milk and butter into potato mixture. Microwave at High uncovered 7 to 10 minutes, or until thickened, stirring several times during cooking.

5 to 15 minutes

1 quart

Soups: Dried Peas, Beans or Lentils

Dried vegetables need water to rehydrate. Notice that the amount of water is the same in both the conventional and microwave versions of this soup. Some evaporation will occur during the 20 to 30 minutes of microwaving.

Conventional soups must be cooked over low heat and stirred to prevent sticking. Since sticking is not a problem in microwaving, the soup can be cooked at High power and stirred only 2 to 4 times. The conventional stirring breaks up the peas, making the soup creamy. If you want to duplicate this consistency in the microwave version, stir more frequently.

Split Pea Soup

2 quarts water
1 lb. (2 cups) green split peas
1½ to 2 lbs. meaty ham bone or 2 cups diced ham
1 medium onion, chopped
½ to 1 teaspoon salt

½ teaspoon basil
¼ teaspoon pepper
1 bay leaf
2 stalks celery, cut into ½-in. slices
2 medium carrots, cut into ¼-in. slices

Makes 2 quarts

In Dutch oven, combine water, split peas, ham bone, onion and seasonings. Bring to boil. Reduce heat to low; cover and simmer 1¼ to 1½ hours, or until peas are tender, stirring occasionally.

Remove bone; cut off meat and dice. Return meat to soup. Add celery and carrots. Cook uncovered over medium-low heat 40 to 50 minutes, or until vegetables are tender and soup is desired thickness, stirring occasionally.

Handwritten annotations: VERY THIN SLICES · ¼ IN. SLICES · 5 QT. CASSEROLE · OMIT · MICROWAVE AT HIGH

Converted Split Pea Soup

2 quarts hot water
1 lb. (2 cups) green split peas
1½ to 2 lbs. meaty ham bone or 2 cups diced ham
1 medium onion, chopped
½ to 1 teaspoon salt
½ teaspoon basil
¼ teaspoon pepper
1 bay leaf
2 stalks celery, cut into ¼-in. slices
2 medium carrots, very thinly sliced

Makes 2 quarts

Combine water, split peas, ham bone, onion and seasonings in 5-qt. casserole. Cover. Microwave at High 40 minutes, stirring several times during cooking.

Remove bone; cut off meat and dice. Return meat to soup. Add vegetables. Microwave, uncovered, 20 to 30 minutes, or until soup is desired thickness and vegetables are tender, stirring several times during cooking.

50 to 90 minutes

1 lb. peas

Sandwiches

Adapting Sandwiches

Most sandwiches adapt easily to microwaving. Pan-grilled sandwiches can be prepared in a browning dish. Oven-broiled sandwiches can be heated in a microwave oven, but will not brown. Stacked, or 3-decker, sandwiches can be adapted, but the layers should be heated side-by-side and assembled after microwaving.

The most common problems with microwaved sandwiches are soggy bread and overheating. Sandwiches which are not made in a browning dish should be wrapped in a paper napkin or placed on a paper towel-lined plate. The paper absorbs steam trapped between the bread and the bottom of the oven.

Toasting bread before microwaving removes excess moisture. A piece of foil placed under the napkin or paper towel will help shield bread on the bottom and keep toast or hard rolls crisp. Heat the bottom of the sandwich and filling first; add the top of a roll or a second slice of toast toward the end of microwaving.

Watch carefully when microwaving cheese. Open the oven door as soon as the cheese softens; it will finish melting from internal heat. If you microwave cheese until it is completely melted, it will be tough and stringy.

Tips for Adapting Sandwiches

Microwave layers side by side when heating stacked sandwiches, so energy can penetrate evenly. If stacked first, the bread will toughen before the center is heated.

Wrap sandwich in paper napkin or place open-face sandwich on towel to absorb steam.

Place foil shield under paper napkin or towel to keep toast and rolls crisp.

Remove cheese-topped sandwiches from oven as soon as cheese softens. Internal heat will complete melting.

Sandwiches: Heated

The procedure for heating sandwiches depends on the amount of filling. Wieners or 3- to 4-oz. of thinly sliced meat may be heated in buns or rolls. Large sausages and dense fillings should be heated first, then placed in rolls and microwaved briefly to warm the bread.

This sample recipe demonstrates the convenience and easy clean-up typical of microwaved sandwiches. The conventional recipe uses three pans; with the microwave version you have one bowl to wash.

Converted Chili-Cheese Dogs

1 can (7½-oz.) chili without beans
4 wieners
4 wiener buns, partially split
2 oz. thinly sliced American cheese

Serves 4

Place chili in small bowl. Microwave at High ¾ to 1½ minutes, or until heated, stirring after half the cooking time.

Place wieners in buns. Arrange on a paper towel-lined plate. Cover with paper towel. Microwave at High 1 to 1½ minutes, or until wieners feel warm to touch, rearranging after half the time.

Spoon chili over wieners. Place cheese on top of chili. Microwave at High ¾ to 1½ minutes, or until cheese melts.

30 seconds to 2 minutes
4 wieners

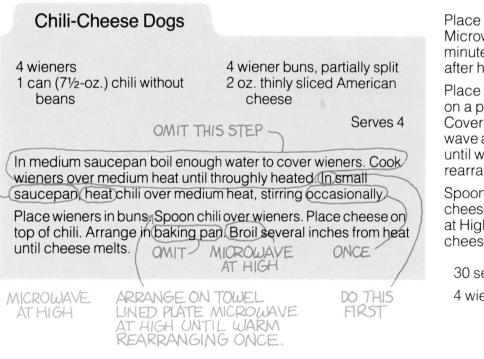

Chili-Cheese Dogs

4 wieners
1 can (7½-oz.) chili without beans

4 wiener buns, partially split
2 oz. thinly sliced American cheese

Serves 4

OMIT THIS STEP

In medium saucepan boil enough water to cover wieners. Cook wieners over medium heat until throughly heated. In small saucepan, heat chili over medium heat, stirring occasionally.

BOWL

Place wieners in buns. Spoon chili over wieners. Place cheese on top of chili. Arrange in baking pan. Broil several inches from heat until cheese melts. *OMIT MICROWAVE ONCE AT HIGH*

MICROWAVE AT HIGH *ARRANGE ON TOWEL LINED PLATE MICROWAVE AT HIGH UNTIL WARM REARRANGING ONCE.* *DO THIS FIRST*

98

Sandwiches: Grilled

The only change necessary to adapt a grilled sandwich for microwaving is to use a preheated browning utensil. If you are making cheese sandwiches, heat from the browning dish may be sufficient to grill the sandwich without further microwaving. Let the sandwich stand in the preheated dish 15 to 20 seconds on the first side. Turn; let stand 20 to 25 seconds. Microwave a few seconds if needed to melt cheese.

Grilled Reuben Sandwiches

Butter or margarine
4 slices pumpernickel or rye bread
4 oz. sliced corned beef

6 tablespoons drained sauerkraut
2 oz. sliced Swiss cheese
1 to 2 tablespoons Thousand Island Dressing

Serves 2

Butter one side of each slice of bread. Place two slices buttered side down on wax paper or a plate. Layer each slice with corned beef, sauerkraut and cheese.

Spread unbuttered side of remaining bread slices with dressing. Place slices, dressing side down, on top of sauerkraut.

Grill sandwiches on both sides in skillet over medium heat until filling is hot and cheese melts.

MICROWAVE AT HIGH

PREHEAT BROWNING DISH

Converted Grilled Reuben Sandwiches

Butter or margarine
4 slices pumpernickel or rye bread
4 oz. sliced corned beef
6 tablespoons drained sauerkraut
2 oz. sliced Swiss cheese
1 to 2 tablespoons Thousand Island Dressing

Serves 2

Butter one side of each slice of bread. Place two slices buttered side down on wax paper or a plate. Layer each with corned beef, sauerkraut and cheese.

Spread unbuttered side of remaining slices of bread with dressing. Place slices dressing side down on top of sauerkraut.

Preheat browning dish 4 minutes at High. Place sandwiches in preheated dish. Microwave 15 to 30 seconds. Turn over; microwave 30 to 45 seconds, or until hot and cheese melts.

Up to 1½ minutes
2 sandwiches

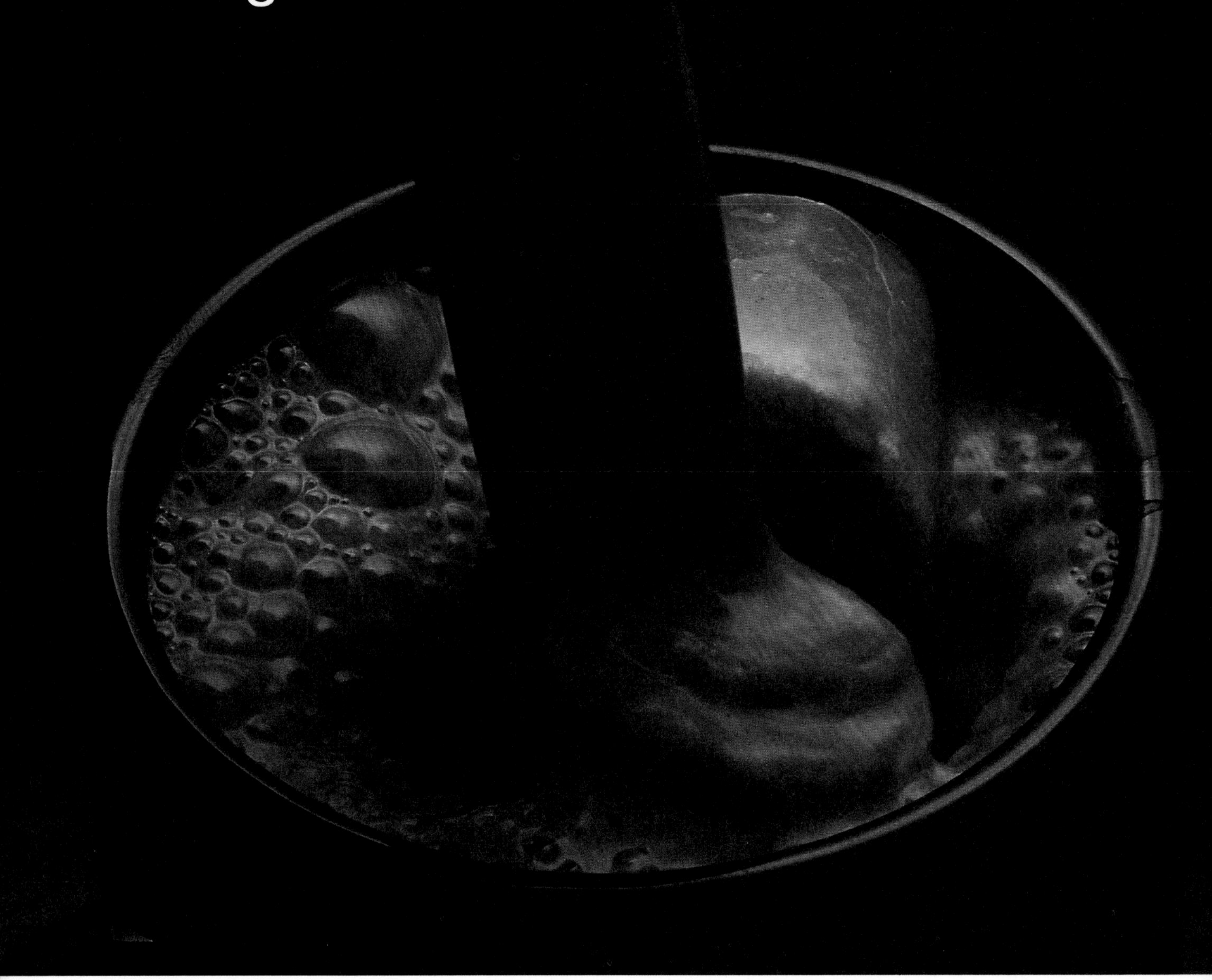

Adapting Beverages

Microwaving speeds and simplifies the preparation of hot beverages. Heat water right in the cup for instant beverages or brewed tea. If you wish to heat water in a teapot, be sure it does not have metalic trim or a metal core inside a rattan-wrapped handle.

Beverages which are cooked, like old-fashioned cocoa or hot lemonade, need no change in ingredients and little or no stirring.

Hot Cocoa

MICROWAVE AT HIGH

CASSEROLE

2½ tablespoons cocoa
  3 tablespoons sugar
    Dash salt — *OMIT*

¼ cup hot water
1¾ cups milk

Serves 2

Combine cocoa, sugar and salt in 1-qt. saucepan. Stir in water until smooth. Heat over medium heat until mixture boils, stirring constantly. Boil 1 minute.

Add milk. Heat through, stirring frequently. Before serving, beat until frothy, if desired. — *OMIT*

NOTE: For richer cocoa, use 3 tablespoons cocoa and 4 tablespoons sugar.

Converted Hot Cocoa

2½ tablespoons cocoa
  3 tablespoons sugar
    Dash salt

¼ cup hot water
1¾ cups milk

Serves 2

Combine cocoa, sugar and salt in 1-qt. casserole. Stir in water until smooth. Microwave at High 45 seconds to 1¼ minutes, or until mixture boils rapidly.

Add milk. Microwave at High 2 to 3½ minutes, or until heated through. Before serving, beat until frothy, if desired.

NOTE: For richer cocoa use 3 tablespoons cocoa and 4 tablespoons sugar.

1 to 4½ minutes   2 servings

Watch and stop cooking before milk boils and forms a skin on top of cocoa.

Sauces

Converting Sauces

Sauces demonstrate the advantages of microwaving. Many of them can be measured, mixed and microwaved in the same container. While different types of sauces vary in the amount of stirring needed, none of them require constant stirring as they do conventionally. Use your microwave oven whenever you need a sauce, even if you prepare the rest of the dish conventionally.

Use a wire whip for stirring. It smooths sauces rapidly and thoroughly even when they are stirred infrequently.

Select a 1-qt. measure or casserole for about 1 cup of liquid. If you double the recipe, select a 2-qt. bowl. Microwaving exaggerates boiling.

Sauces: Thickened with Flour

The modern method of making a conventional white or brown sauce thickened with flour is to stir the sauce constantly until it has boiled 1 minute. Since the conventional sauce does not reduce significantly during cooking, the microwave version needs no change in ingredients. The only diference is in the amount of stirring.

Some classic sauce recipes call for simmering an hour or two after the sauce has thickened. To convert this type of recipe, use a little more flour. After the sauce has thickened, reduce power to 50% (Medium) and microwave uncovered 20 to 30 minutes, stirring once or twice.

Pan Gravy

3 tablespoons fat from
   drippings
3 tablespoons flour

1¼ cups liquid (au jus,
   water, milk, broth)
Bouquet sauce, optional
Salt and pepper

Makes about 1½ cups

[handwritten: OMIT]

In frying pan, combine hot fat and flour over medium heat. Cook until bubbly. Slowly stir in liquid. Cook over medium-high heat until thick, stirring often.

If desired, add a few drops of bouquet sauce for color. Salt and pepper to taste.

[handwritten annotations: 1 QT. CASSEROLE — STIRRING AFTER 2 MINUTES, THEN EVERY MINUTE. — MICROWAVE AT HIGH]

Converted Pan Gravy

3 tablespoons fat from
   drippings
3 tablespoons flour
1¼ cups liquid (au jus, water,
   milk, broth)
Bouquet sauce, optional
Salt and pepper

Makes about 1½ cups

In 1-qt. casserole combine hot fat and flour. Blend in liquid. Microwave at High 5 to 8 minutes, or until thickened, stirring after 2 minutes and then every minute with fork or wire whip.

Add a few drops of bouquet sauce for color, if desired. Salt and pepper to taste.

4 to 9½ minutes

1¼ to 1¾ cups

Sauces: Thickened with Cornstarch

Sauces made with cornstarch thicken more rapidly and need less stirring than flour-based sauces. In this sample recipe, sugar was blended with cornstarch before hot water was added. The sauce was not stirred during cooking.

If your recipe does not call for sugar, dissolve the cornstarch in ¼ cup cool water before adding the remaining liquid. Stir the sauce well with a wire whip after 2 minutes of microwaving.

How to Blend Cornstarch

Blend cornstarch with sugar in sweet sauces before stirring in hot liquid.

Dissolve cornstarch in ¼ cup cold water to prevent lumping of non-sweet sauces.

Converted Lemon Sauce

 2 tablespoons cornstarch
½ cup sugar
   Dash salt
 1 cup hot water
 2 tablespoons butter or
    margarine
 2 tablespoons lemon juice
 2 teaspoons grated lemon rind

Makes 1½ cups

In 1-qt. measure, blend together cornstarch, sugar and salt. Add water, stirring until sugar dissolves. Microwave at High 2 to 5 minutes, or until sauce is clear and thick. Stir with wire whip or fork. Mix in remaining ingredients. Serve warm or cool.

1½ to 5½ minutes

1¼ to 1¾ cups

Lemon Sauce

 2 tablespoons cornstarch
½ cup sugar
   Dash salt
 1 cup hot water

 2 tablespoons butter or
    margarine
 2 tablespoons lemon juice
 2 teaspoons grated lemon rind

Makes 1½ cups

USE 1 QT. MEASURE

In medium saucepan, stir together cornstarch, sugar and salt. Slowly blend in water. Cook over medium heat until sauce is clear and thick, stirring constantly. Remove from heat.

Stir in remaining ingredients. Serve warm or cool.

MICROWAVE
AT HIGH.

Sauces: Thickened with Egg Yolk

Use these guidelines for white or veloute' sauces enriched with egg yolks. If your conventional recipe calls for mixing the egg yolk and liquid together before thickening, follow the microwave method given here. It is important to stir some of the hot mixture into the egg yolk so that it heats gradually before it is added to the sauce. The flour in the sauce stabilizes the egg, so it can be microwaved at High power without curdling.

How to Blend Egg Yolk with Sauce

Microwave white or veloute' sauce until thickened.

Stir half the sauce into slightly beaten egg yolk gradually.

Blend egg yolk mixture into remaining sauce with whip.

Cooked Salad Dressing

2 tablespoons flour
1 tablespoon sugar
½ teaspoon salt
½ teaspoon dry mustard
¾ cup milk
1 egg yolk, slightly beaten
3 tablespoons vinegar
1 tablespoon butter or
   margarine

Makes 1 cup

Combine flour, sugar, salt and dry mustard in 1-qt. saucepan. Gradually stir in milk. Heat over medium heat until boiling, stirring constantly. Boil 1 minute while stirring.

Gradually stir half of the hot mixture into egg yolk. Blend this into remaining mixture. Boil 1 minute stirring constantly. Remove from heat; add vinegar and butter. Cool slightly; refrigerate.

MICROWAVE
AT HIGH

USE
CASSEROLE

EVERY
MINUTE

MICROWAVE AT
HIGH, STIRRING ONCE.

Converted Salad Dressing

2 tablespoons flour
1 tablespoon sugar
½ teaspoon salt
½ teaspoon dry mustard
¾ cup milk
1 egg yolk, slightly beaten
3 tablespoons vinegar
1 tablespoon butter or
   margarine

Makes 1 cup

Combine flour, sugar, salt and dry mustard in 1-qt. casserole. Gradually stir in milk. Microwave at High 3 to 5 minutes, or until mixture thickens, stirring every minute.

Gradually stir half the hot mixture into egg yolk. Blend into remaining mixture in casserole. Microwave at High 1½ to 2½ minutes, or until mixture thickens, stirring after half the time. Add vinegar and butter. Cool slightly; refrigerate.

1¼ to 3½ minutes
¾ to 1¼ cups

Sauces: Cheese

Cheese sauce is made by adding grated cheese to a thickened white or veloute' sauce. The only changes needed are a microwave method and time. In the conventional recipe, cheese is stirred into the sauce while it is still on the stove. In the microwave version, cheese is stirred into the hot sauce, which is returned to the oven for a few seconds if necessary, to complete melting.

Cheese Sauce

2 tablespoons butter or
  margarine
2 tablespoons flour
¼ teaspoon salt

⅛ teaspoon pepper
1 cup milk
1 cup shredded Cheddar
  cheese

Makes 1½ cups

Melt butter in 1-qt. saucepan. Blend in flour and seasonings. Gradually stir in milk.

Cook over medium heat until mixture boils and thickens, stirring constantly. Stir in cheese until melted. Remove from heat.

MICROWAVE AT HIGH.   *CASSEROLE*   *EVERY MINUTE*

Sauces: Hollandaise

Sauces from the hollandaise family are made of egg yolks thickened with butter over very low heat. They are more difficult to convert than other sauces because they require a special microwaving method. If you try to follow the conventional method, the egg yolks will scramble before the butter melts. For microwaving, the butter must be melted but not hot. Add the yolks to the butter and microwave at 50% (Medium) to prevent curdling.

Hollandaise Sauce

3 egg yolks
2 tablespoons lemon juice
½ cup butter or margarine

¼ teaspoon salt
Dash cayenne pepper

Makes ⅔ cup

Combine egg yolks and lemon juice in top of double boiler, beat with wire whip. Add ⅓ butter to egg yolk mixture and cook over hot, not boiling, water, stirring constantly until butter melts. Repeat with another ⅓ of butter. Repeat with remaining butter, beating until mixture thickens.

Remove from heat. Stir in remaining ingredients.

MELT ALL THE BUTTER ADD YOLK MIXTURE   *SMALL BOWL*   *MICROWAVE AT 50% (MEDIUM) STIRRING EVERY 30 SECONDS.*

How to Adapt & Microwave

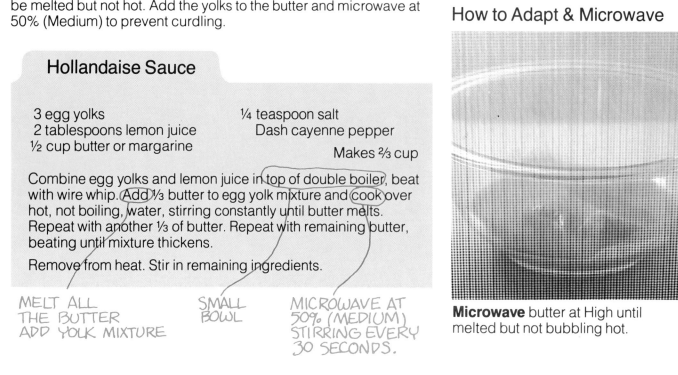

Microwave butter at High until melted but not bubbling hot.

106

Converted Cheese Sauce

2 tablespoons butter or margarine
2 tablespoons flour
¼ teaspoon salt
⅛ teaspoon pepper
1 cup milk
1 cup shredded Cheddar cheese

Makes 1½ cups

Melt butter in 1-qt. casserole at High, 30 to 50 seconds. Blend in flour and seasonings. Gradually stir in milk.

Microwave 4 to 6½ minutes or until mixture boils and thickens, stirring every minute.

Stir in cheese until melted. Microwave 15 to 20 seconds if needed.

3¼ to 7 minutes

Depends on amount of ingredients, form and temperature of cheese.

Converted Hollandaise Sauce

3 egg yolks
2 tablespoons lemon juice
¼ teaspoon salt
   Dash cayenne pepper
½ cup butter or margarine

Makes ⅔ cup

In small bowl, blend all ingredients except butter.

In small bowl, microwave butter at High 45 seconds to 1 minute, or until melted. With wire whip, stir egg yolk mixture into butter.

Microwave at 50% (Medium) 45 seconds to 1¾ minutes, or until sauce is desired consistency, stirring every 30 seconds and watching closely when sauce begins to thicken. Blend with wire whip before serving.

30 seconds to 2 minutes

½ to 1 cup

Hollandaise Sauce

Stir egg yolk mixture into butter with wire whip.

Reduce power to 50% (Medium). Microwave until thickened, stirring every 30 seconds.

Vegetables & Salads

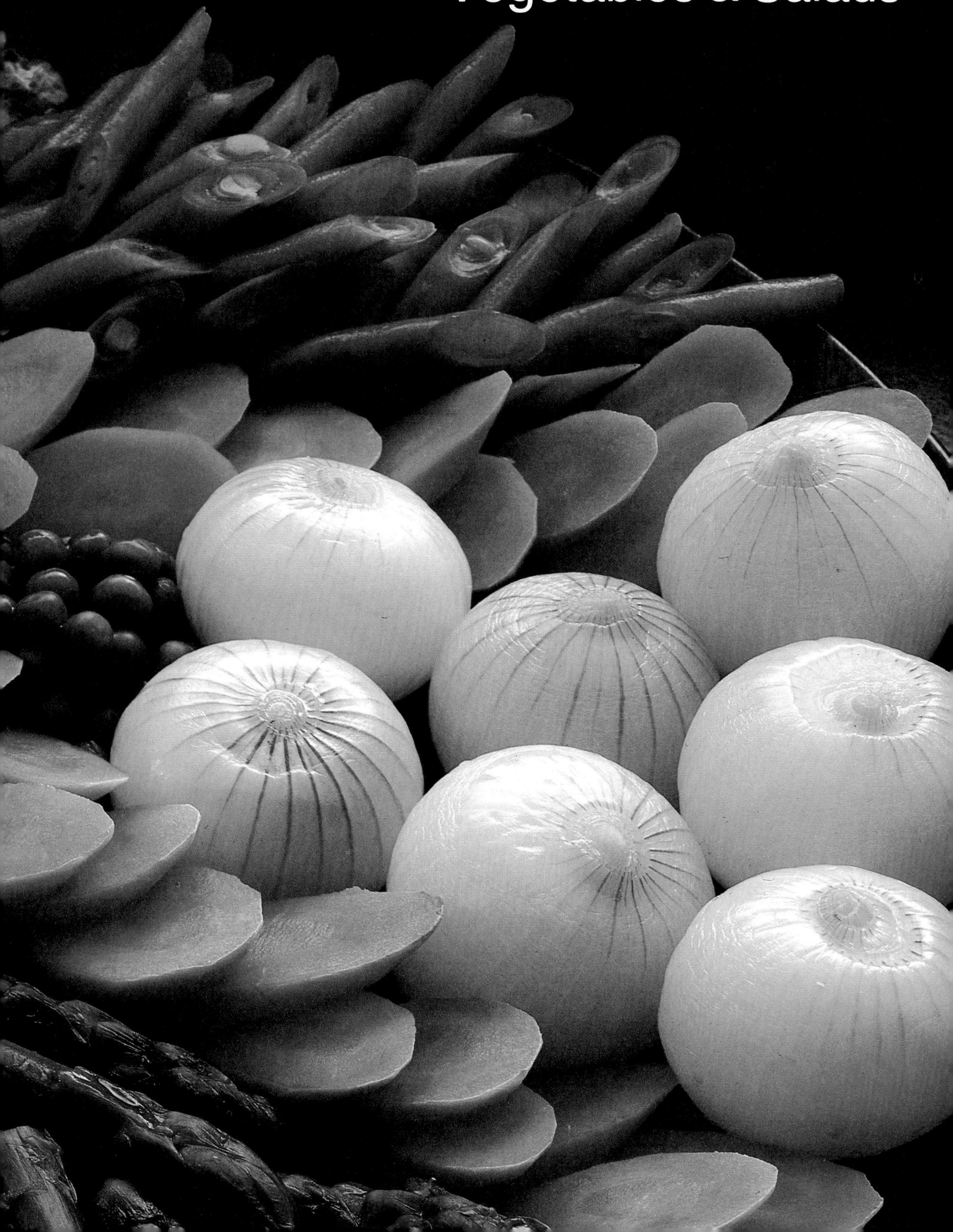

Adapting Vegetables

Microwave vegetables for maximum flavor and nutrition. Many vegetables can be cooked in their own natural moisture, or with a few tablespoons of water to provide steam. Since vitamins and minerals are water soluable, less water means less loss of food value.

Consult a microwave cookbook or vegetable cooking chart when converting vegetable combinations. Add quick-cooking vegetables toward end of microwaving. Remember that total cooking time depends on the amount as well as type of vegetable.

Standing time is an important part of vegetable microwaving. It prevents overcooking of large, dense vegetables, like winter squash, or vegetables with delicate ends like asparagus, broccoli or cauliflowerets.

How to Adapt Vegetable Recipes

Use very little water. Some vegetables require no water, especially when the recipe contains butter or oil.

Add quick-cooking vegetables toward the end when microwaving several types together, so all will be done at the same time.

Allow ample standing time to complete cooking of large, whole vegetables.

Standing time equalizes doneness of vegetables which have delicate tips.

Some Things That Don't Work and Why

Casseroles layered with bread are unsatisfactory because the bread absorbs moisture from the vegetables rather than staying crisp as it does conventionally. Crumb toppings are excellent.

Vegetables: Uncooked

Some of the advantages of microwaving vegetables are improved flavor, texture and appearance. If your recipe calls for liquid, reduce it. Many vegetables microwave in their own natural moisture. Consult a microwave cookbook or chart for the amount of water needed for specific vegetables.

In the microwave version of this recipe, the vegetables retain their individual shapes and attractive color. Conventionally, the tomatoes provide moisture to cook the other vegetables. When microwaving, we reserved the tomatoes for part of the cooking time since they are needed only for color and flavor. Use the same procedure with fresh tomatoes and other quick-cooking ingredients.

Ratatouille

SLICE THINLY

2 medium zucchini, cut into
¼-in. slices
2 medium onions, cut into
¼-in. slices and
separated into rings
1 medium eggplant, peeled
and cut into ¾-in. cubes
¼ cup olive or salad oil
1 teaspoon basil
1 teaspoon oregano
1 teaspoon parsley flakes
½ teaspoon sugar
½ teaspoon salt
⅛ teaspoon pepper
⅛ teaspoon garlic powder
1 can (16-oz.) tomatoes,
drained and cut in half

Serves 6 to 8

ADD TOMATOES LATER   *CASSEROLE*
Combine all ingredients except tomatoes in Dutch oven or 3-qt. casserole. Gently stir in tomatoes. Cover and simmer over medium heat 20 to 25 minutes, or until vegetables are tender, stirring occasionally. — *ONCE*   *MICROWAVE AT HIGH*

Converted Ratatouille

2 medium zucchini, cut into
¼-in. slices
2 medium onions, thinly sliced
and separated into rings
1 medium eggplant, peeled
and cut into ¾-in. cubes
¼ cup olive or salad oil
1 teaspoon basil
1 teaspoon oregano
1 teaspoon parsley flakes
½ teaspoon sugar
½ teaspoon salt
⅛ teaspoon pepper
⅛ teaspoon garlic powder
1 can (16-oz.) tomatoes,
drained and cut in half

Serves 6 to 8

Combine all ingredients except tomatoes in 3-qt. casserole. Cover. Microwave at High 8 minutes. Gently stir in tomatoes and re-cover.

Microwave 12 to 15 minutes, or until vegetables are tender, stirring after half the cooking time.

10 to 18 minutes

1½ to 2½-qts.

Vegetables: Pre-cooked

Casseroles made with pre-cooked vegetables need little or no change except for microwave method and time. When you are not using canned ingredients, save precious nutrients and time by using your microwave oven to cook or defrost vegetables.

If your casserole is very saucy or bakes for a long time, reduce the amount of liquid slightly. It will not evaporate during the short microwaving time.

This sample recipe is a dense custard, and takes time to bake conventionally. No change in ingredients was needed to convert it. To microwave, we started at High, then reduced power to 50% (Medium). Since the casserole could not be stirred, we rotated the dish ¼ turn during microwaving. A brief standing time completes cooking. Notice the amount of time saved.

Orange Yam Bake

MICROWAVE AT HIGH

1½ to 2 lbs. yams, (cooked) and peeled or 1½ lbs. canned yams, drained
¼ cup butter
1 egg
¼ cup chopped pecans, optional
3 tablespoons undiluted orange juice concentrate
2 tablespoons brown sugar

½ teaspoon cinnamon
¼ teaspoon nutmeg
¼ teaspoon vanilla
⅛ teaspoon salt

Topping:
2 tablespoons brown sugar
1 tablespoon flour
1 tablespoon butter or margarine
¼ cup chopped pecans

Serves 4 to 6

OMIT

(Preheat) oven to 375°.

In medium mixing bowl, whip potatoes with electric mixer. (Melt) butter in small (saucepan.) Blend into potatoes. Add remaining ingredients, except topping, mix well. Pour potato mixture into 1-qt. casserole.

In small bowl, mix together topping ingredients until well-blended and crumbly. Sprinkle topping over potatoes. (Bake 40 to 50 minutes, or until heated through and set. (Center will remain somewhat creamy.)

USE / CUP MEASURE

MICROWAVE AT HIGH, THEN 50% (MEDIUM) ROTATING DISH.

MICROWAVE AT HIGH.

Converted Orange Yam Bake

1½ to 2 lbs. yams, cooked*
 and peeled or 1½ lbs.
 canned yams, drained
¼ cup butter
1 egg
¼ cup chopped pecans,
 optional
3 tablespoons undiluted
 orange juice
 concentrate
2 tablespoons brown sugar
½ teaspoon cinnamon
¼ teaspoon nutmeg
¼ teaspoon vanilla
⅛ teaspoon salt

Topping:
2 tablespoons brown sugar
1 tablespoon flour
1 tablespoon butter or
 margarine
¼ cup chopped pecans

Serves 4 to 6

In medium mixing bowl, whip potatoes with electric mixer.

In 1 cup measure, microwave butter at High 30 to 45 seconds, or until melted. Stir into potatoes. Blend remaining ingredients, except topping, into potatoes. Pour into 1-qt. casserole.

In small bowl, mix together topping ingredients until well-blended and crumbly. Sprinkle topping over potatoes.

Microwave at High 3 minutes. Reduce power to 50% (Medium). Microwave 8 to 14 minutes, or until heated through and set. (Center will remain somewhat creamy), rotating ¼ turn once during cooking. Let stand 3 to 5 minutes.

*To microwave: Wash and pierce potatoes. Microwave at High 13 to 19 minutes, or until potatoes yield to pressure, rearrange once. Let stand 5 minutes.

6 to 18 minutes
1½ to 2¼ lbs. yams

Vegetables: Stuffed

Peppers, eggplant, onions, acorn squash or zucchini stuffed with rice or a vegetable combination make an intriguing side dish. With the addition of cooked meat, poultry or fish, they become economical and satisfying main dishes.

When the filling is precooked, the stuffed vegetable should take about the same time as it does when whole. Dense vegetables, like acorn squash, should be partially cooked before stuffing. Actual microwaving time depends on the number, type and size of vegetables.

In this sample recipe, the zucchini needed no change except microwaving method and time. They hold their shape better than conventionally cooked. If your recipe includes a sauce, reduce the amount by about half.

Stuffed Zucchini

2 medium zucchini	½ teaspoon salt ·
½ cup cooked rice	¼ teaspoon basil
¼ cup chopped onion	1 small tomato, peeled,
¼ cup chopped green pepper	seeded and chopped

Serves 4

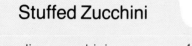

─OMIT
~~Preheat~~ oven to 375°.

Cut zucchini in half lengthwise. Scrape out pulp, leaving a ¼-in. shell. Chop pulp and combine with rice, onion, green pepper, salt and basil.

DISH

Place zucchini shells in 8×8-in. ~~pan.~~ Mound ¼ of vegetable mixture into each shell. Top with chopped tomato. ~~Cover~~ and bake 25 to 35 minutes, or until shells are ~~tender.~~

ROTATE ½ TURN
AFTER 3 MINUTES.

WITH
WAX PAPER

How to Prepare Vegetables for Stuffing

Remove top, seeds and pith from peppers.

Microwave whole onions for about half the cooking time before hollowing out centers. When onions are cool enough to handle, centers will be easy to remove.

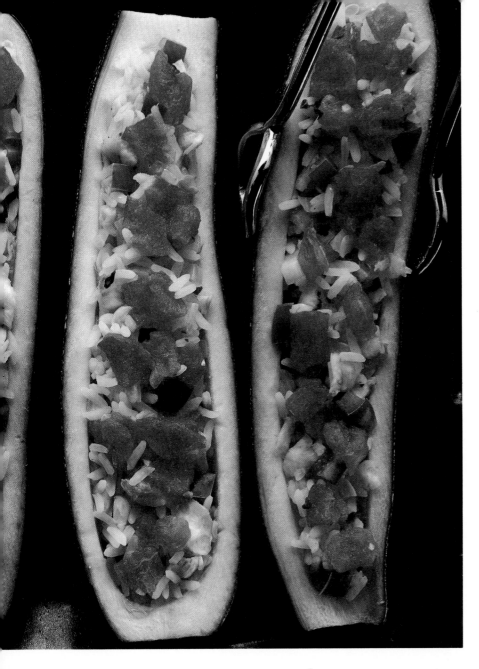

Converted Stuffed Zucchini

2 medium zucchini
½ cup cooked rice
¼ cup chopped onion
¼ cup chopped green pepper
½ teaspoon salt
¼ teaspoon basil
1 small tomato, peeled, seeded and chopped

Serves 4

Cut zucchini in half lengthwise. Scrape out pulp, leaving a ¼-in. shell. Chop pulp and combine with rice, onion, green pepper, salt and basil.

Place zucchini shells in 8×8-in. dish. Mound ¼ of vegetable mixture into each shell. Top with chopped tomato. Cover with wax paper. Microwave at High 5 to 7 minutes, or until shells are tender, rotating dish ½ turn after 3 minutes.

NOTE: If recipe calls for parboiled zucchini, microwave at High 1 to 2 minutes, or until warm and softened, before cutting.

4 to 10 minutes
2 medium zucchini

Halve zucchini or eggplant lengthwise. Use grapefruit knife or spoon to remove center, leaving a ½-in. shell. Chop pulp and add to filling.

Microwave whole squash for half the cooking time. Halve it and scrape out seeds.

Vegetables: Dried Beans, Peas & Lentils

Dried vegetables need water to rehydrate, so you should not reduce liquid when converting a conventional recipe. They also require time to tenderize, so the cooking time is almost the same. Microwaved beans look more attractive because they keep their shape and are not broken up with frequent stirring.

We tried converting traditional New England baked beans and found that the microwaved beans were firmer and more glazed than conventionally cooked. Some of our testers preferred their flavor and texture, but felt they would not satisfy people who are used to soft or mushy baked beans. If your recipe calls for more than 2 or 3 hours of baking, there would be a time advantage in microwaving. However, the beans are more like conventionally cooked when allowed to stand 24 hours after cooking.

Beans in Tomato Sauce

1 lb. Northern beans	**Sauce:**
6 cups water	3 onions, chopped
3 celery stalks (tops only)	2 cloves garlic, minced
1 onion	¼ cup butter or margarine
5 sprigs parsley	3 tablespoons flour
4 cloves garlic	1½ cups hot water
2 teaspoons basil leaves	2 teaspoons instant chicken
1 teaspoon thyme leaves	bouillon granules
1 teaspoon salt	½ can (6-oz.) tomato paste
½ teaspoon pepper	½ teaspoon pepper

5 QT. CASSEROLE   *MICROWAVE AT 50% (MEDIUM)*   Serves 6 to 8

In a Dutch oven, combine beans and water. Let stand overnight, or heat water and beans to boiling. Boil 2 minutes. Remove from heat; cover and let stand 1 hour.   *CASSEROLE*

Add remaining ingredients except sauce. (If desired, tie parsley, garlic, basil and thyme in cheesecloth for easy removal.) Simmer, covered, for 1 hour, or until beans are tender but not soft. Drain and reserve liquid. Remove seasonings. Let beans stand covered.

In 2-qt. saucepan, saute onions and garlic in butter until tender. Blend in flour. Stir in remaining ingredients. Simmer 20 minutes, stirring often.

Add sauce to beans in Dutch oven. Simmer, covered, for 1 hour, or until beans are soft, stirring often. Add reserved liquid to beans as needed while cooking.

MICROWAVE AT HIGH.

5 QT. CASSEROLE STIRRING ONCE OR TWICE

MICROWAVE AT HIGH.

How to Microwave Beans

Use the full amount of water to soften and microwave beans.

Converted Beans in Tomato Sauce

1 lb. Northern beans
6 cups water
3 celery stalks (tops only)
1 onion
5 sprigs parsley
4 cloves garlic
2 teaspoons basil leaves
1 teaspoon thyme leaves
1 teaspoon salt
½ teaspoon pepper

Sauce:

3 onions, chopped
2 cloves garlic, minced
¼ cup butter or margarine
3 tablespoons flour
1½ cups hot water
2 teaspoons instant chicken
    bouillon granules
½ can (6-oz.) tomato paste
½ teaspoon pepper

Serves 6 to 8

In a 5-qt. casserole, combine beans and water. Let stand overnight, or microwave at High 8 to 10 minutes, or until water boils. Boil 2 minutes. Let stand 1 hour.

Add remaining ingredients except sauce. (If desired, tie parsley, garlic, basil and thyme in cheesecloth.) Microwave covered at 50% (Medium) 45 minutes to 1 hour, or until beans are tender but not soft. Drain and reserve liquid. Remove seasonings. Let beans stand, covered.

In 2-qt. casserole, microwave onions, garlic and butter at High 4 to 7 minutes, or until onion is tender. Blend in flour. Add remaining ingredients. Microwave at High 10 to 15 minutes, or until thickened, stirring once or twice.

Add sauce to beans in 5-qt. casserole. Microwave covered at High 50 minutes to 1 hour, or until beans are soft, adding reserved liquid as needed, stirring 3 or 4 times.

Combine beans and sauce, which will be somewhat thinner than conventional mixture. Less reserved bean liquid will be needed during the final microwaving.

2 to 4 hours

1 lb. beans

Salads

Use your microwave to speed cooking of chicken, bacon and vegetables for salad combinations. Guidelines for adapting cooked salad dressing are on page 105.

Hot salads need only a microwave cooking method and time to adapt them. You'll save time and effort because microwaving requires less stirring.

For this sample recipe, we microwaved the potatoes in only ¼ cup of water, which improves nutrition and flavor. Compare the microwave and conventional cooking times.

To microwave the bacon, we used a rack set in a 12×8-in. dish, which collects the drippings. If you don't have a removable rack, place the bacon directly in the dish.

Notice the difference in stirring required. The potatoes do not break up as readily in the microwave version because they need not be stirred during heating.

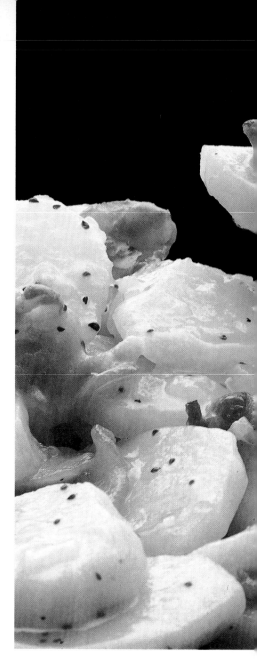

German Potato Salad

[handwritten: MICROWAVE AT HIGH, REARRANGING ONCE.]

[handwritten: ¼ CUP]
Water *[handwritten: REDUCE]*
2 teaspoons salt, divided
4 medium potatoes, peeled
    and cut in half
4 slices bacon
1 medium onion, chopped

2 tablespoons sugar
1 tablespoon flour
¼ teaspoon celery seed
    Dash pepper
½ cup water
¼ cup vinegar

Serves 4 to 6

[handwritten: 2 QT. CASSEROLE]

In large saucepan, heat 1-in. water and 1 teaspoon salt to boiling. Add potatoes. Heat to boiling. Reduce heat to medium. Cover and cook 20 to 25 minutes, or until fork tender. Drain. Set aside.

[handwritten: OMIT]
In 10-in. skillet, fry bacon until crisp. Drain bacon on paper towels. Add onion to bacon fat and cook over medium heat until tender, stirring occasionally. Stir in sugar, flour, 1 teaspoon salt, celery seed and pepper.

Cook over low heat until bubbly, stirring constantly. Mix in water and vinegar. Heat to boiling, sitrring constantly. Boil and stir 1 minute. Remove from heat.

[handwritten: ONCE]
Crumble bacon into hot mixture, then slice in potatoes. Cook over meidum-low heat until hot and bubbly, stirring gently.

[handwritten: USE RACK IN 12X8 IN. DISH.]   *[handwritten: MICROWAVE AT HIGH]*   *[handwritten: MICROWAVE AT HIGH, COVERED WITH PAPER TOWEL.]*

How to Adapt & Microwave

Microwave potatoes in only ¼ cup of water.

Converted German Potato Salad

¼ cup water
1½ teaspoons salt, divided
4 medium potatoes, peeled and cut in half
4 slices bacon
1 medium onion, chopped
2 tablespoons sugar
1 tablespoon flour
¼ teaspoon celery seed
Dash pepper
½ cup water
¼ cup vinegar

Serves 4 to 6

Combine water and ½ teaspoon salt in 2-qt. casserole. Add potatoes. Cover. Microwave at High 10 to 14 minutes, or until fork tender, rearranging after half the cooking time. Set aside.

Place bacon on rack in 12×8-in. dish. Cover with paper towel. Microwave at High 3 to 4 minutes, or until bacon is crisp. Drain bacon on paper towels.

Remove rack from dish. Add onion to bacon fat. Microwave 1½ to 2½ minutes, or until onion is tender.

Stir in sugar, flour, 1 teaspoon salt, celery seed and pepper. Microwave 45 to 60 seconds, or until mixture starts to bubble. Stir in water and vinegar. Microwave 4 to 6 minutes, or until mixture thickens, stirring after half the cooking time.

Crumble bacon into hot mixture, then slice in potatoes. Stir gently. Microwave 1 to 2 minutes, or until heated through.

15 to 25 minutes

4 medium potatoes with sauce

German Potato Salad

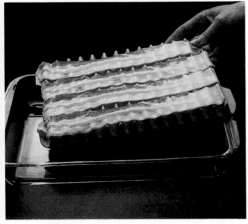

Cook bacon on rack in baking dish to catch drippings.

Make sauce in baking dish. Add bacon and potatoes. Heat and serve in same dish.

Breads & Baking

Adapting Yeast Breads

Microwaved breads do not brown, so you will want to select recipes which contain whole grains for color or can be finished with a topping or icing. Absence of browning is an advantage if you are baking white bread for sandwich loaves or canapes; there won't be any crust to trim.

Shortening. Yeast dough for microwaving needs extra shortening to prevent toughness and dryness. Use about ¼ cup shortening for 2½ to 3 cups of flour.

Toppings. Crumbs for topping breads and lining loaf dishes can be made from leftover dried bread, cake and cookies as well as crackers, cereals and snack chips. Brush shaped bread or rolls with melted butter or milk before rolling in toppings. Use butter with bread crumbs and sugar mixtures. Milk is preferred with coarser toppings because the coating adheres better. Coat bread and rolls heavily since the surface expands about 3 times during final rising and baking.

Proofing. Even when you bake bread conventionally you can use the microwave for proofing (rising) if you have a 10% (Low) setting. For the final rising, be sure to use a dish which suits both types of oven. Directions for proofing dough are on page 124.

Microwave-Baking. Microwave yeast breads at 50% (Medium). Loaf shapes should be rotated at least once; every 3 minutes is a good guide. Rotate rolls and coffeecakes every 2 minutes.

Tips for Adapting Yeast Breads

Use at least ¼ cup shortening for 2½ to 3 cups of flour.

Brush bread or rolls with milk or melted butter to help toppings adhere to surface.

Coat surface generously, because it expands during rising and baking.

Toppings for Yeast and Quick Breads

Bread, rolls and biscuits
Wheat germ, wheat flakes or cracked wheat
Oatmeal or cornmeal
Plain or seasoned bread crumbs

Soda, snack crackers, rye crisps, flat breads or chow mein noodles, crumbed
Potato or other chips, melba toast or croutons, crushed

Crumbs combined with Parmesan cheese, herbs or seeds such as poppy, sesame or caraway

Converting Quick Breads

Quick breads can be mixed and baked immediately; they do not need time to rise. There are many types of quick breads. The guidelines for adapting and microwaving them depends upon the type of bread.

Muffins. Add 1 to 2 tablespoons more shortening for each cup of flour. Use 2 cupcake liners for each muffin to absorb excess moisture. Fill liners ⅓ full. Use a topping on light colored muffins. Microwave in a ring as directed for cupcakes, page 133.

Biscuits. Microwave biscuits do not brown. Before baking, dip them in melted butter and coat with crumbs. Microwave biscuits as directed below until they are firm to the touch.

Fruit and Nut Loaves. Chop fruit and nuts finely. Batters thin out at the start of microwaving so large pieces would sink. Add 1 to 2 tablespoons more shortening. Microwave quick breads rise higher and do not mound in the center.

A recipe calling for 1¼ to 1⅓ cups of flour makes a full loaf. With a larger recipe, fill the dish ⅓ to ½ full and bake remaining batter as cupcakes.

Coffeecakes. Add 1 or 2 more tablespoons of shortening. Reduce baking powder by about ¼. Coffeecakes which have heavy toppings or a "topping" mixture in the bottom of the pan should be set on an inverted saucer. Microwave as directed for layer cakes.

Tips for Converting Quick Breads

Increase shortening by 1 to 2 tablespoons. Cornbread will need even more; biscuits require no change.

Fill dishes or cupcake liners ⅓ to ½ full to allow for higher rising.

Arrange biscuits in a ring around a plate, leaving space for extra rising. Rotate plate after half the cooking time.

Muffins, sweet rolls, coffeecakes. Graham cracker crumbs, Chopped nuts, Crumbed Sweet rolls, coffeecake, cookies, dried cake or muffins, Cinnamon-sugar.

Some Things That Don't Work and Why

French Bread and Hard Rolls do not form a crisp crust.

Popovers need hot, dry air to form crusty sides.

Waffles and Pancakes must be baked on a hot surface.

Doughnuts cannot be deep-fried in the microwave oven because fat becomes dangerously hot.

Yeast Bread

Yeast breads need little change in ingredients other than increased shortening. Grease dishes lightly, then sprinkle with one of the dry products suggested for bread toppings on page 122. This absorbs excess moisture which forms between the bread and the dish during microwaving. It also provides color and texture.

This sample recipe calls for wheat germ in the dough, so we used wheat germ to prepare the pans, too. You may also coat the entire loaf with a bread topping. If your oven does not have a setting of 10% (Low), let the bread rise (proof) as you would conventionally in a warm place free from drafts.

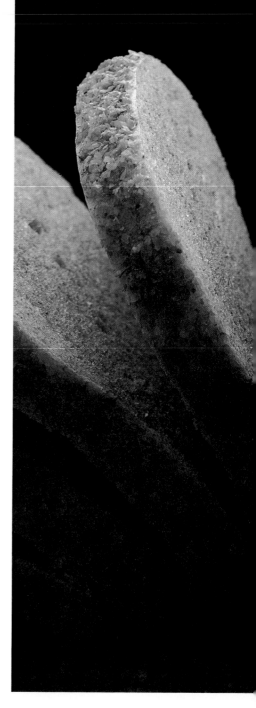

Whole Wheat Bread

2 cups milk, divided
2 pkgs. dry yeast
½ cup honey
¼ cup wheat germ
2 tablespoons butter or margarine

1½ teaspoons salt
2½ to 3 cups all-purpose flour
2½ cups wheat flour

Makes 2 loaves

[handwritten annotations: INCREASE 1 CUP MEASURE; USE WHEAT GERM TO "FLOUR" DISH]

In medium saucepan, heat ½ cup milk until lukewarm. Mix with yeast in small bowl to dissolve yeast. Set aside.

In large mixing bowl, combine honey, wheat germ, butter and salt. Scald remaining milk. Pour over honey mixture, stirring to blend. Let cool until lukewarm. Add yeast mixture. Add white and wheat flour 1 cup at a time, beating with each addition, until stiff dough forms. Turn onto floured board. Knead until dough is elastic.

Form into ball. Place dough in lightly greased bowl, turn once. Cover with light towel and set in warm place until doubled in bulk (1½ to 2 hours). Turn out on floured board. Divide into 2 loaves. Shape loaves to fit two lightly greased 9×5-in. pans. Place in pans. Cover. Let stand in warm place until doubled in bulk.

Preheat oven to 400°. Bake bread for 15 minutes. Reduce heat to 350°. Bake 40 to 45 minutes, or until loaves sound hollow when tapped. Remove from pans. Cool on rack. *DISHES*

[handwritten annotation: OMIT]

[handwritten annotations: MICROWAVE AT HIGH. | MICROWAVE AT 50% (MEDIUM). | MICROWAVE AT 10% (LOW) ROTATING ONCE.]

How to Adapt Yeast Breads for Microwaving

Measure and scald milk in the same cup.

Proof dough with 1 cup water in oven at 10% (Low) power.

Press finger into dough lightly. When doubled, print remains.

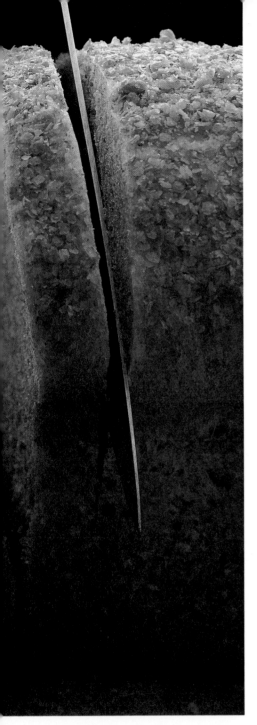

Converted Whole Wheat Bread

2 cups milk, divided
2 pkgs. dry yeast
½ cup honey
¼ cup wheat germ
¼ cup butter or margarine

1½ teaspoons salt
2½ to 3 cups all-purpose flour
2½ cups wheat flour
Wheat germ

Makes 2 loaves

In 1 cup measure, microwave ½ cup milk at High 30 to 40 seconds, or until lukewarm. Stir in yeast to dissolve. Set aside.

In large mixing bowl, combine honey, wheat germ, butter and salt. In 2 cup measure, microwave remaining milk at High 2 to 3¼ minutes, or until scalded. Pour over honey mixture. Stir to blend. Let stand until lukewarm. Add yeast mixture. Add white and wheat flour 1 cup at a time, beating with each addition, until stiff dough forms. Turn onto floured board. Knead until dough is elastic.

Form into ball. Place dough in lightly greased bowl, turn once. Cover with light towel. Place in oven with 1 cup warm water. Microwave at 10% (Low) 12 to 18 minutes, or until doubled in bulk. Rotate dish once, checking for uneven heat on dough.

Place dough on floured board. Divide into 2 loaves. Lightly grease two 9×5-in. loaf dishes. Dust dishes with wheat germ on bottom and sides. Shape loaves to fit dishes. Place in dishes.

Cover with paper towels or light towels. Proof bread with 1 cup of warm water in oven, one loaf at a time, by microwaving at 10% (Low) 12 to 18 minutes, or until doubled in bulk. Rotate dish halfway through, checking for warm spots on dough. (If dough begins to get too warm, each loaf can be proofed for half the total time, then finished after resting, alternating loaves.) Repeat with remaining loaf.

To cook bread: Remove water from oven, uncover loaves. Microwave, one loaf at a time, at 50% (Medium) 4 to 8 minutes, or until top springs back to touch.

Remove from dish. Brush with butter. Sprinkle with wheat germ and poppy seeds, if desired.

4 to 14 minutes

Cooking time for 1 loaf

Dust lightly greased dish with dry topping, page 122.

Proof shaped loaves 1 at a time at 10% (Low) power.

Microwave 1 loaf at a time at 50% (Medium) power until done.

Quick Bread

The amount of change needed in quick bread ingredients depends on the individual recipe. Decrease the liquid in dense batters by about 2 tablespoons. Very liquid batters will require a greater reduction. Increase shortening by approximately 2 tablespoons or more if the batter is not rich.

In this sample recipe, the batter is very moist, so we reduced the liquid by ⅓ and added a second egg as a binder. Since corn bread is not rich, our first attempt was crumbly when baked, so we increased the shortening by 4 tablespoons rather than 2.

Corn Bread

REDUCE   INCREASE

1 cup flour
1 cup yellow corn meal
2 tablespoons sugar
4 teaspoons baking powder

½ teaspoon salt
1 cup milk
¼ cup shortening
1 egg

Serves 9

Preheat oven to 425°.

In medium mixing bowl combine flour, corn meal, sugar, baking powder and salt. Add milk, shortening and egg. Beat until fairly smooth, about 1 minute. DISH

Grease an 8×8-in. baking pan. Pour batter into pan. Bake 20 to 25 minutes, or until center springs back when touched. LET STAND

OMIT

MICROWAVE AT 50% (MEDIUM) THEN HIGH, ROTATING ONCE.

Converted Corn Bread

1 cup flour
1 cup yellow corn meal
2 tablespoons sugar
4 teaspoons baking powder

½ teaspoon salt
⅔ cup milk
½ cup shortening
2 eggs

Serves 9

In medium mixing bowl combine flour, corn meal, sugar, baking powder and salt. Add milk, shortening and eggs. Beat until fairly smooth, about 1 minute.

Pour batter into ungreased 8×8-in. dish. Microwave at 50% (Medium) 6 minutes, rotating dish after half the cooking time. Increase power to High. Microwave 2 to 5 minutes, or until center springs back when touched. Let stand directly on counter 5 minutes.

6 to 15 minutes

One loaf

How to Microwave Quick

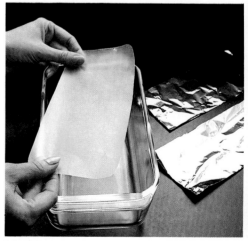

Line bottom of glass dish with wax paper. Shield ends of dish with foil.

Bread Loaves

Elevate dish on saucer. Microwave at 50% (Medium), then High.

Rotate loaf ¼ turn every 3 minutes. Remove foil during last couple of minutes.

Check doneness through bottom of dish. No unbaked batter should appear in center bottom.

Desserts

Converting Scratch Cakes

Microwaved cakes rise higher and are airier than conventionally baked. They do not brown, but this difference is not apparent when the cake is frosted or served with a topping.

Shapes. Round and ring shapes bake most evenly. Shield the corners of a square dish with triangles of foil to reduce the energy received in these areas. Do not use a rectangular baking dish unless your oven manufacturer recommends it.

Dish Preparation. You may grease dishes lightly, but do not flour them. The flour will bake onto the surface of the cake. If the cake is to be turned out before serving, line the dish with a piece of wax paper cut to fit the bottom.

Cake Size. Because microwaved cakes rise higher, fill dishes no more than half full. If your recipe calls for more than one cup of flour per layer, you will have extra batter which you can bake as cupcakes.

Selecting Recipes. The best cakes for microwave conversion are rich cakes using whole eggs. Oil cakes, other than chiffon, are good choices. If the cake is not rich, increase shortening by about 2 tablespoons.

Microwave cakes are very tender. To make them less fragile, add an extra egg and reduce liquid by about 2 tablespoons. Cakes which contain 3 or more eggs can be adjusted by reducing the liquid even more, if you do not care to add more eggs. Cut liquid by ⅓ if the cake is baked in layers, and ¼ or less if you choose a ring shape.

Microwaving. Start the cake at 50% (Medium) and rotate the dish during cooking. This will give the cake a more even surface.

Increase power to High for the final baking period. Actual microwaving time at each power setting and the frequency of rotation depends on the type and size of the cake.

High Altitude. If you live at a high altitude, your microwave cakes will rise even higher. Follow the guidelines above for recipes already changed for conventional high altitude baking.

If you are converting a new recipe, follow your usual high altitude procedures. In general, we suggest decreasing liquid by 2 tablespoons per cup, sugar by 1 to 2 tablespoons per cup, and leavening by ¼ teaspoon for each teaspoon. Add 2 more tablespoons of flour for each cup. Microwaving time at 50% (Medium) will be slightly longer.

How to Adapt Cakes

Add an extra egg and reduce liquid by about 2 tablespoons.

Reduce liquid by approximately ¼ to ⅓ if your recipe already contains 3 or more eggs.

Increase shortening if the recipe contains less than ⅓ cup for each cup of flour.

Round cakes microwave evenly. Bake one layer at a time.

Ring shapes allow energy to penetrate from center as well as top, bottom and sides.

Square cakes need shielding with foil in the corners. Remove foil when you increase power to High for final baking period.

Test moist spots by touching them. If moisture comes off on your finger, leaving surface dry, cake is done.

Fill dishes no more than half full. Unless you have special deep sided cake dishes for microwaving, make a few cupcakes when the recipe calls for more than 1 cup of flour per layer.

Line dish with wax paper if cake is to be turned out for frosting and serving. Place dish on paper, mark a line around outside, then cut inside the line and fit paper into dish.

Some Things That Don't Work and Why

White cakes toughen because egg whites do not contain sufficient fat.

Angel and Sponge cakes require dry heat.

Chiffon cakes must be especially formulated for microwave baking.

Sheet cakes cook unevenly. Bake as layers.

Cakes: Layer

Rich, moist yellow, chocolate or spice cakes convert well for microwaving. Add an extra egg to a 1- or 2-egg cake. For a 3-egg cake, reduce the liquid by approximately ⅓.

White cakes are less suitable for microwaving, but can be converted by changing from a white to a yellow cake. Substitute 1 whole egg for 2 egg whites.

Mix the batter as your conventional recipe directs, but fill the dishes only half full. If you do not have deep sided cake dishes made especially for microwaving, use 9-in. dishes or bake the extra batter as cupcakes. Microwave layers one at a time.

This chocolate cake already contained three eggs, so we reduced the liquid, using a convenient measurement which was close to ⅓. Layer cake recipes can also be converted to tube shapes by following the guidlines on page 135. We tested this chocolate cake in a ring mold, using 1 cup of liquid.

MICROWAVE TO MELT.

REDUCE

Chocolate Layer Cake

1⅔ cups flour	2 squares unsweetened
1¼ cups buttermilk	chocolate, melted and
1 cup sugar	slightly cooled
½ cup brown sugar	1½ teaspoons baking soda
½ cup shortening	1 teaspoon salt
3 eggs	1 teaspoon vanilla

Makes 2 layers

OMIT

Preheat oven to 350°. Grease and flour two 8- to 9-in. round layer pans. Combine all ingredients in large mixing bowl. Beat at low speed until ingredients are blended. Beat at high speed 3 minutes, scraping bowl frequently.

Pour batter into pans. Bake 30 to 35 minutes, or until center springs back when lightly touched. Cool 5 to 10 minutes on rack before removing from pan.

USE DISHES

MICROWAVE 1 LAYER AT A TIME, AT 50% (MEDIUM) AND HIGH, ROTATING ONCE DURING EACH COOKING PERIOD.

LINE WITH WAX PAPER

ON COUNTER

NO MORE THAN HALF FULL

Tips for Microwaving Cakes

Melt chocolate in small bowl at 50% (Medium) 3½ to 5 minutes, stirring after half the time.

Converted Chocolate Layer Cake

1⅔ cups flour
¾ cup buttermilk
1 cup sugar
½ cup brown sugar
½ cup shortening
3 eggs
2 squares unsweetened chocolate, melted and slightly cooled
1½ teaspoons baking soda
1 teaspoon salt
1 teaspoon vanilla

Makes 2 layers

Line two 8- to 9-in. round layer dishes with wax paper. Combine all ingredients in large mixing bowl. Beat at low speed until ingredients are blended. Beat at high speed 3 minutes, scraping bowl frequently.

Pour batter into dishes, filling no more than half full.*

Microwave one layer at a time at 50% (Medium) 6 minutes, rotating dish after half the cooking time. Increase power to High. Microwave 2 to 5 minutes, or until center springs back when lightly touched, rotating after half the cooking time. Let stand directly on counter top 5 to 10 minutes before removing.

*If using 8-in. cake pans there will be batter left for approximately 6 cupcakes. Microwave at High 2 to 3 minutes for 6 cupcakes.

Microwave cake at 50% (Medium), then High, rotating once during each cooking period.

Place cupcakes in ring. Microwave 2 to 3 minutes at High, rearranging after half the time.

6 to 12 minutes
One layer

133

Cakes: Bundt or Tube

The ring shape is excellent for microwaving because energy penetrates from all sides of the ring. With the exception of white cakes, layer cake recipes can be microwaved in a ring-shaped dish. Angel, sponge and chiffon cakes cannot be converted for microwaving. This sample recipe is a white cake which we changed to a yellow cake by using whole eggs. We added the eggs at the beginning of mixing, as we would with a yellow cake recipe.

When converting a ring-shape cake, be sure your mold is large enough so batter will fill it no more than half full. Grease the dish lightly, but do not flour it. Chopped nuts may be sprinkled in the bottom of the dish to provide a topping when cake is turned out.

Reduce liquid slightly. The reduction is not as great for a ring cake as it is for a layer or square cake because of the longer microwaving time.

Start the cake at 50% (Medium) power for ⅔ to ¾ of the total microwaving time, then finish at High power. Rotate the cake once during each cooking period.

Let the cake stand directly on the counter, so trapped heat will complete cooking of the bottom. Notice that the standing time is shorter than for a conventional cake.

Ring Cake

REDUCE (milk) — USE 3 WHOLE EGGS. (egg whites)

2 cups flour
1½ cups sugar
1 cup milk
¼ cup shortening
¼ cup butter or margarine
3½ teaspoons baking powder
1 teaspoon salt
1 teaspoon vanilla
6 egg whites

Makes one cake

Preheat oven to 350°. Grease and flour a 12-cup bundt pan.

Combine all ingredients except egg whites in large mixing bowl. Beat at low speed until blended. Beat at high speed 1½ minutes, scraping bowl frequently. Add egg whites and continue beating 1½ minutes, scraping bowl frequently.

Pour batter into pan. Bake ~~45 to 55 minutes,~~ or until top springs back when lightly touched. Cool 20 minutes upright in pan on a baking rack before removing.

OMIT (Preheat) — OMIT (flour) — DISH (pan) — INCLUDING WHOLE EGGS (except egg whites) — OMIT (Add egg whites) — 10 TO 15 (20) — DIRECTLY ON COUNTER (baking rack) — MICROWAVE AT 50% (MEDIUM) AND HIGH ROTATING TWICE (Bake)

Converted Ring Cake

2 cups flour
1½ cups sugar
¾ cup milk
3 eggs
¼ cup shortening
¼ cup butter or margarine
3½ teaspoons baking powder
1 teaspoon salt
1 teaspoon vanilla

Makes one cake

Lightly grease a 12-cup microwave bundt dish.

Combine all ingredients in large mixing bowl. Beat at low speed until ingredients are blended. Beat at high speed 3 minutes, scraping bowl frequently.

Pour batter into dish. Microwave at 50% (Medium) 12 minutes, rotating after half the cooking time. Increase power to High. Microwave 3½ to 6½ minutes, or until top springs back when lightly touched, rotating after half the cooking time. Let stand 10 to 15 minutes upright in dish directly on counter top before removing.

12 to 20 minutes

One cake

Tips for Microwaving Ring Cake

Cut through batter with knife to eliminate air bubbles.

Glaze cake with ½ cup orange marmalade that has been microwaved at High 20 to 45 seconds until melted.

Converting Pies

Pre-baked shell. All micro-waved pies start with a pre-baked shell. If the pastry is not baked first, it may absorb moisture from the filling and be soggy and undercooked. Micro-wave the crust until it is dry and opaque before adding and microwaving the filling.

Browning. Microwaved pastry is exceptionally tender and flaky, but it does not brown. Add 3 to 4 drops of yellow food coloring to the water when mixing pie dough. This gives it an attractive color.

Preparing crust. 9-in. pie plates differ in size. Some measure less than 9 inches across the top, while others are shallow.

Microwaving exaggerates boil-ing, so fruit and custard fillings cooked in the shell may bubble over if the shell is not large enough. A high fluted rim will help contain bubbling. Micro-wave any extra filling in a custard cup. Prick pie crust with a fork in a continuous line at the bend of the dish. Then prick the bottom and sides at ½-in. intervals.

Microwaving crust. Microwave the shells as directed on page 89. If the crust is cooking unevenly, rotate ¼ turn every minute. The crust is done when it appears dry and flaky. With a glass pie plate, check through the bottom for doneness.

Liquid fillings. Some pie fillings are very liquid and may seep through the prick holes before they thicken. If this is a problem, seal the prick holes before filling the shell. With a soft brush gently brush a well-beaten egg yolk over the holes. Microwave at High 30 seconds to set the egg.

To convert pumpkin and other custard pies, follow the directions for Quiche, page 88. In that recipe the custard is partially cooked before it is poured into the precooked shell; seepage is not a problem because the filling has already started to thicken.

How to Make a High Fluted Rim for Microwave Pies

Roll out pastry 2-in. larger than inverted pie plate. Fit dough into plate without stretching.

Fold overhang to make a standing rim. Push pastry into a V-shape at ½-in. intervals.

Pinch flutes to make sharp edges. Prick crust generously with a fork to eliminate shrinking.

Some Things That Don't Work and Why

Double-crust Pies cannot be microwaved because the bottom crust does not cook properly.

How to Microwave Pie Crusts

Plain microwaved pastry looks cooked but does not brown. One way to give it color is to mix 3 to 4 drops of yellow food coloring with the water when preparing dough.

Microwave pie shell first. It should be dry and flaky before filling is added.

Check for doneness a minute before the minimum time, since crusts differ in thickness and moisture content. Pastry should be dry and opaque. a few lightly browned spots may appear.

Seal prick holes with beaten egg yolk before adding and micro-waving very liquid fillings.

Crumb Crusts adapt to microwaving without change in ingredients. Use graham crackers, chocolate or vanilla wafers, or ginger snaps. Melt butter right in pie plate. Stir in crumbs and sugar, if used. Press crumbs firmly against bottom and sides of plate. Microwave 1½ minutes, rotating ½ turn after 1 minute.

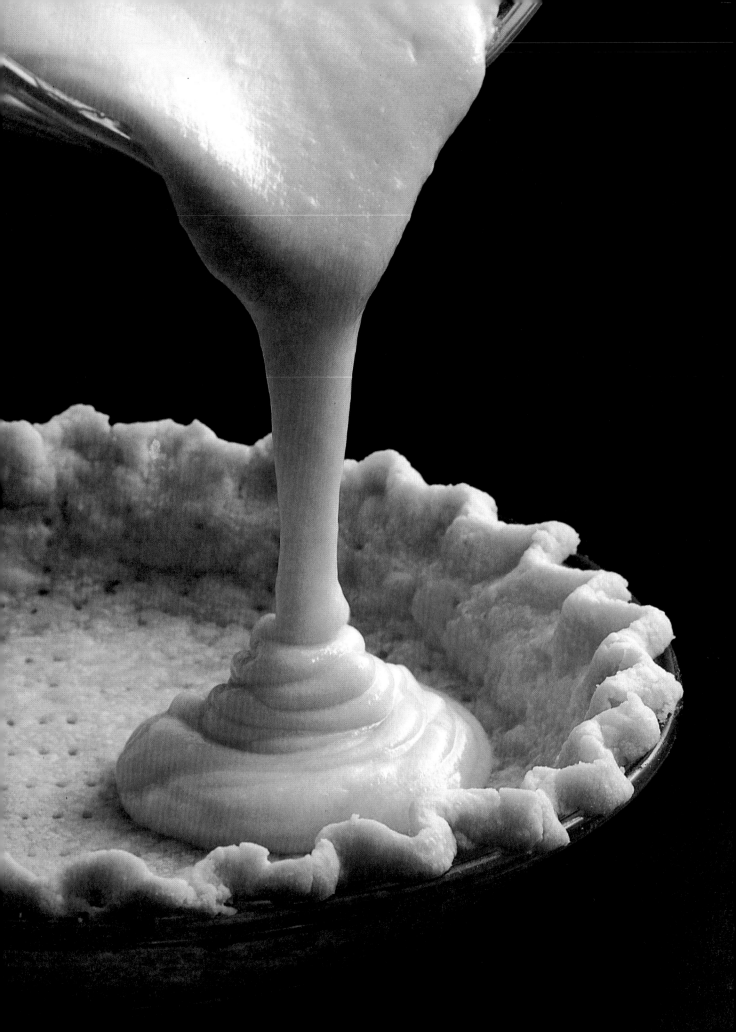

Pies: Cream, Chiffon or Marshmallow

These pies adapt easily to microwaving because the crust and filling are cooked separately. Microwaving speeds and simplifies preparation of the fillings.

For a chiffon pie, combine gelatin and other ingredients to be cooked in a small bowl. Microwave at High 1 to 2 minutes, or until gelatin melts and is slightly thickened. If mixture contains egg yolks, use 50% (Medium) power and increase the time by 1 to 2 minutes.

To prepare marshmallow fillings, combine marshmallows and other ingredients to be heated in a casserole. Microwave at High 2 to 4 minutes, stirring every minute, until marshmallows melt.

This sample recipe is for a cream pie. The only difference is the microwave method and time. The microwave version needs far less stirring. Use a wire whip for best results. If you are adapting an old-fashioned double-boiler recipe, you'll appreciate microwave ease and speed even more.

Vanilla Cream Pie

[handwritten: MICROWAVE]

⅔ cup sugar
¼ cup cornstarch
½ teaspoon salt
3 cups milk
4 egg yolks, slightly beaten

2 tablespoons butter or margarine
1 tablespoon plus 1 teaspoon vanilla
1 baked 9-in. pie shell

One 9-inch pie

[handwritten: MICROWAVE AT HIGH] *[handwritten: 3 OR 4 TIMES]*

In medium saucepan, blend sugar, cornstarch and salt. Stir in milk. Cook over medium heat, stirring constantly, until mixture thickens and boils. Boil for 1 minute, stirring constantly. Stir some of the hot mixture into egg yolks. Blend yolk mixture into remaining hot mixture. Boil over medium heat for 1 minute, stirring *[handwritten: OMIT]* constantly. Remove from heat. Stir in butter and vanilla until butter melts. Pour into baked pie shell. Refrigerate 2 hours, or until set.

NOTE: Place plastic wrap on top of filling as it cools to prevent "skin" from forming.

Converted Vanilla Cream Pie

⅔ cup sugar
¼ cup cornstarch
½ teaspoon salt
3 cups milk
4 egg yolks, slightly beaten
2 tablespoons butter or margarine
1 tablespoon plus 1 teaspoon vanilla
1 baked 9-in. pie shell, page 89

One 9-inch pie

In 2-qt. mixing bowl, blend sugar, cornstarch and salt. Add milk, stirring until well mixed. Microwave at High 8 to 12 minutes, or until thick, stirring with wire whip 3 or 4 times.

Stir some hot mixture into egg yolks. Blend egg yolk mixture into remaining hot mixture. Microwave at High 1 minute.

Blend in butter and vanilla, stirring until butter melts. Pour into baked pie shell. Refrigerate 2 hours, or until set.

NOTE: Place plastic wrap on top of filling as it cools to prevent "skin" from forming.

7 to 13 minutes

Cream pie filling for one pie

How to Make Smooth Cream Fillings

Blend a little of hot milk mixture into egg yolks to warm them slightly.

Combine egg yolk mixture and remaining hot milk mixture, using the wire whip.

Stir milk and cornstarch mixture with a wire whip 3 or 4 times during microwaving.

Fruit Pies

Microwave fruit pies have a superior fresh fruit flavor because of the short cooking time. They differ from most conventional pies because the shell must be pre-baked and they do not have a top crust. Instead of a crust, we made pastry cut-outs from leftover dough and used them to decorate the finished pie. A streusel topping could be used.

The difference in actual size of pie plates labeled "9-in." is important with fruit pies because they bubble high when microwaved. If your plate measures 9-in. across and is 1½-in. deep, the full amount of filling will fit. With a smaller plate, use less fruit or bake the extra filling separately in a custard cup.

A high fluted rim helps contain bubbling. As an extra precaution, place a sheet of wax paper on the bottom of the oven. If the pie bubbles very hard during microwaving, reduce the power setting to 70% (Medium-high) or 50% (Medium). Add extra time if necessary.

Actual microwaving time depends on the type of fruit used. Apples take longest. Check berry pies after 10 minutes. The pie is done when the filling is hot and has started to cook in the center. It will cook more as it cools to serving temperature.

Crisps and Crumbles are microwaved the same as fruit pie fillings. Follow conventional directions for mixing and topping them, but use a microwave dish and time. The topping on adapted cobblers will not brown. Microwave fruit for about ¼ the time, top with biscuits and microwave until they are firm to the touch and fruit is tender.

Apple Pie

REDUCE, ADD 3 TO 4 DROPS OF YELLOW FOOD COLORING

Pastry:
⅔ cup shortening
3 to 4 tablespoons butter or margarine
2 cups all-purpose flour
1 teaspoon salt
6 tablespoons cold water

Filling:
¾ cup sugar
¼ cup flour
½ teaspoon ground nutmeg
½ teaspoon ground cinnamon
Dash salt
6 cups sliced, peeled apples

9-inch pie

MIXED WITH FOOD COLORING

Cut shortening and butter into flour and salt with a pastry cutter until particles resemble coarse crumbs.

Sprinkle water over pastry while stirring with a fork, until dough is just moist enough to hold together. Divide in half, form into 2 balls. Set one half aside.   *GENEROUS   OMIT*

Flatten remaining dough to ½-in. Roll out on floured pastry cloth to scant ⅛-in. thick circle, 2-in. larger than inverted 9-in. pie pan. Fit loosely into pie pan. Trim edges to ½-in. Set aside.

Mix all filling ingredients, except apples, in a bowl. Add apples and toss to coat. Turn into pie shell.

Roll remaining dough into ⅛-in. thick circle. Place over pie and seal to bottom crust. Flute edges. Slit top crust.

Bake 40 to 50 minutes, or until juices bubble through slits.

OMIT

MICROWAVE AT HIGH UNTIL APPLES ARE TENDER. ROTATE ONCE. DECORATE WITH CUT-OUTS.   MICROWAVE SHELL AND CUT-OUTS AT HIGH.

How to Microwave

Roll scraps of dough out to ⅛-in. thick. Cut into 6 designs with cookie cutter.

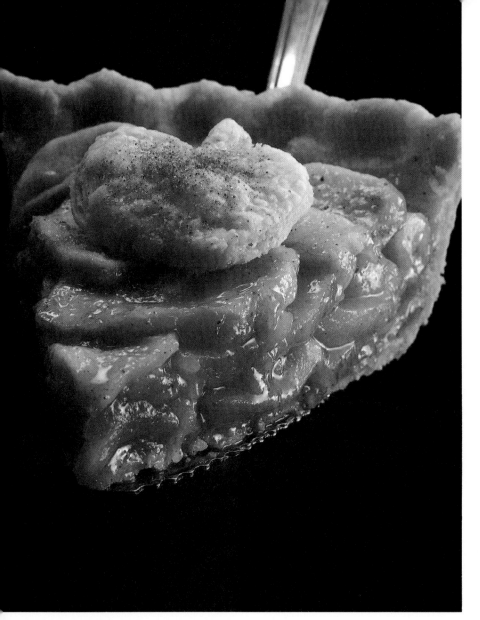

Converted Apple Pie

Pastry:
⅓ cup shortening
1 to 2 tablespoons butter or
    margarine
1 cup all-purpose flour
½ teaspoon salt
2 to 3 tablespoons cold water
3 to 4 drops yellow food coloring

Filling:
¾ cup sugar
¼ cup flour
½ teaspoon ground nutmeg
½ teaspoon ground cinnamon
    Dash salt
6 cups sliced, peeled apples

9-inch pie

Cut shortening and butter into flour and salt with a pastry cutter until particles resemble coarse crumbs. Combine water and food coloring. Sprinkle over pastry while stirring with a fork, until dough is just moist enough to hold together.

Flatten dough to ½-in. Roll out on floured pastry cloth to scant ⅛-in. thick circle, 2-in. larger than inverted 9-in. pie plate. Fit loosely into 9-in. pie plate. Trim overhang to generous ½-in. Fold to form a standing rim and flute.

Microwave at High 6 to 7 minutes, rotating dish ½ turn after 3 minutes. Cool.

Make pastry cut-outs following picture directions.

Mix all filling ingredients, except apples, in a bowl. Add apples; toss to coat. Turn into pie shell.

Place sheet of wax paper in bottom of oven. Microwave pie at High 14 to 18 minutes, or until apples are tender, rotating dish ½ turn after 8 minutes. Decorate with pastry cut outs.

16 to 30 minutes

9-in. pie

Pastry Cut-outs

Arrange cut-outs in ring on microwave baking sheet or wax paper. Sprinkle with mixture of 1 teaspoon sugar and ⅛ teaspoon cinnamon.

Microwave at High 2 to 4 minutes, or until dry and puffy, rotating after 2 minutes. Set aside.

Converting Cookies

Most bar cookies convert well for microwaving except those which contain a high proportion of shortening. The fat becomes hot rapidly and melts over the batter, causing parts of it to overcook.

A full batch of individual cookies baked on a sheet may take longer to microwave because fewer can be baked at a time. Their texture may be different from conventional cookies.

When you bake cookies conventionally, test a few in the microwave oven. You'll soon learn which ones are suitable. Cookies may bake more evenly if the microwave baking sheet is elevated as directed on page 20.

Meringue drops get crisper and harder when microwaved. Icebox cookies may spread more than conventionally baked.

The best choices are stiff, crumbly batters with more flour in proportion to shortening, such as oatmeal or peanut butter drops. Molded cookies, like Russian or Swedish tea cakes, work very well, as do sugar cookies which are not too buttery. Since cookies do not brown, choose those which do not require browning, have natural color, are frosted or sugared.

Tips for Converting Cookies

Bar Cookies adapt easily and are microwaved in far less time than conventional baking.

Shield corners with foil to prevent overcooking or drying.

Cool bars directly on a heat-proof countertop before removing them from dish.

Crumbly, stiff doughs hold their shape best when you are microwaving individual cookies.

Choose cookies which are not supposed to brown, like Swedish tea cakes, or have colored batters, like brownies and spice drops. Frosting and powdered or colored sugar add eye and appetite appeal.

Some Things That Don't Work and Why

Cake-style Drop Cookies are too soft to hold their shape.

Bars

Bar cookies are more frequently adapted for microwaving than other types. Since they do not brown, you may want to finish light-colored cookies with a frosting or topping.

While a round dish is ideal for microwaving, most people prefer square bars. The corners of square dishes receive more energy during microwaving, so we recommend shielding to prevent drying or overcooking in these areas.

Rotate bar cookies twice during microwaving. Dense batters, like brownies, which require longer cooking, should be rotated more often. Fudgy brownies should stand 30 minutes on countertop to complete cooking.

Peanut Butter Oatmeal Bars

6 tablespoons peanut butter, divided
¼ cup sugar
¼ cup brown sugar
3 tablespoons shortening
1 egg
½ teaspoon vanilla
½ cup flour
½ cup quick-cooking rolled oats
¼ teaspoon baking soda
¼ teaspoon salt
½ cup semi-sweet chocolate chips

Makes 24

Preheat oven to 350°. Lightly grease an 8×8-in. baking pan.

In medium mixing bowl cream together 4 tablespoons peanut butter, sugar, brown sugar, shortening, egg and vanilla until fluffy.

Stir together dry ingredients. Add to creamed mixture and beat well. Spread batter in pan. Bake 15 to 20 minutes. Cool.

In small saucepan combine chocolate chips and remaining peanut butter. Melt over very low heat, stirring constantly. Frost bars.

(handwritten annotations:) OMIT — OMIT — DISH — SHIELD CORNERS — BOWL — MICROWAVE AT 50% (MEDIUM) — MICROWAVE AT HIGH, ROTATING ¼ TURN TWICE.

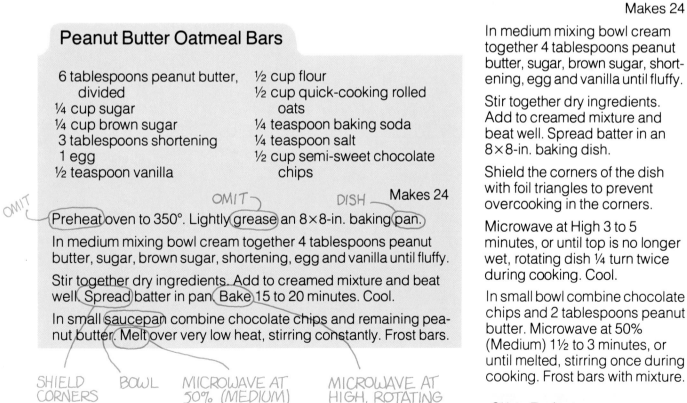

Converted Peanut Butter Oatmeal Bars

6 tablespoons peanut butter, divided
¼ cup sugar
¼ cup brown sugar
3 tablespoons shortening
1 egg
½ teaspoon vanilla
½ cup flour
½ cup quick-cooking rolled oats
¼ teaspoon baking soda
¼ teaspoon salt
½ cup semi-sweet chocolate chips

Makes 24

In medium mixing bowl cream together 4 tablespoons peanut butter, sugar, brown sugar, shortening, egg and vanilla until fluffy.

Stir together dry ingredients. Add to creamed mixture and beat well. Spread batter in an 8×8-in. baking dish.

Shield the corners of the dish with foil triangles to prevent overcooking in the corners.

Microwave at High 3 to 5 minutes, or until top is no longer wet, rotating dish ¼ turn twice during cooking. Cool.

In small bowl combine chocolate chips and 2 tablespoons peanut butter. Microwave at 50% (Medium) 1½ to 3 minutes, or until melted, stirring once during cooking. Frost bars with mixture.

2½ to 7 minutes

Similar amount ingredients

Adapting Candy

Most conventional candies require constant stirring during part of their preparation. Microwaving simplifies candy making. The only change needed to adapt conventional recipes is microwave method and time.

Be sure to use a large enough container. Sugar attracts microwave energy, so the mixtures boil high. Caramels boil up very high when stirred. We do not recommend them unless you use great care.

Do not use a conventional candy thermometer in the microwave oven. You may use a thermometer to check candies, but it must be put in as soon as you open the oven door to get an accurate reading.

Microwave Candy Thermometer registers up to 320° and can be used in oven during microwaving.

How to Test Candy for Doneness

Unless you have a microwave oven-safe thermometer which registers up to 320°, the old-fashioined cold water test is the best way to judge doneness of microwaved candies. Fill a small cup with very cold tap water. Drop about ½ teaspoon of candy mixture into the water. Let stand a few seconds, then test with fingers.

Thread (230° to 234°). Syrup spins a 2-in. thread as it drops from spoon.

Soft Ball (234° to 240°). Mixture can be shaped into soft ball, but flattens on removal from water.

Firm Ball (244° to 248°). Mixture forms a firm ball which does not flatten when removed from water.

Hard Ball (250° to 266°). Mixture forms a hard, but pliable ball.

Soft Crack (270° to 290°). Syrup separates into hard but not brittle threads.

Hard Crack (300° to 310°). Syrup separates into hard and brittle threads.

Toffee

Conventional toffee must be stirred constantly to prevent scorching. In the microwave version, butter is cut into chunks to speed melting, and the mixture is stirred 3 to 6 times. Use a larger container and check color and consistency each time you stir to avoid overcooking.

Toffee

handwritten: CUT IN CHUNKS

1 cup chopped pecans
¾ cup brown sugar
½ cup butter or (margarine) *circled*

½ cup semi-sweet chocolate
 chips
        Makes 1 pound

handwritten: MICROWAVE AT HIGH.

Spread pecans evenly in buttered 8×8-in. pan.

In 1-qt. saucepan, heat sugar and butter to boiling over medium heat, stirring constantly. Boil for 7 minutes, stirring constantly.

Spread mixture evenly over nuts in pan. Sprinkle chocolate chips over candy. Let stand 20 seconds until chocolate is melted. Spread chocolate over candy. Cool. Break into pieces.

handwritten: 2 QT. SAUCE PAN
handwritten: STIRRING AFTER 2 MINUTES, THEN EVERY MINUTE.

Converted Toffee

1 cup chopped pecans
¾ cup brown sugar
½ cup butter or margarine, cut in chunks
½ cup semi-sweet chocolate chips
        Makes 1 pound

Spread pecans evenly in buttered 8×8-in dish or pan. In 2-qt. casserole, combine sugar and butter. Microwave at High 4½ to 8½ minutes, or until sugar is dissolved, stirring after 2 minutes then every minute. Do not overcook.
Spread mixture over nuts in dish. Sprinkle with chocolate chips. Let stand 20 seconds until chocolate is melted. Spread chocolate over candy. Cool. Break into pieces.

3½ to 11 minutes

Similar amount ingredients

How to Microwave Toffee

Use a casserole larger than the pan needed conventionally. This prevents over-boiling.

Stir after 2 minutes, then every minute, rather than constantly as the conventional recipe directs.

Microwave toffee until sugar is dissolved and mixture looks smooth, not grainy, with a rich, golden brown color.

Fudge

Microwaving modernizes the making of old-fashioned fudge. Since the sugar does ot need constant stirring until it dissolves, the casserole can be covered for the first 5 minutes to speed melting of chocolate and sugar. After the cover is removed, the fudge is stirred only 3 times. Notice that a larger container is needed to prevent boil over. Use the traditional soft-ball test to check for doneness.

Fudge

2 cups sugar
1 cup milk
2 squares unsweetened
   chocolate
1 tablespoon light corn
   syrup

⅛ teaspoon salt
2 tablespoons butter or
   margarine
1 teaspoon vanilla
½ cup chopped nuts,
   optional

Makes 1 pound

Butter a 9×5-in. or 10×6-in. loaf pan; set aside.

Butter the sides of a 2-qt. *(3 QT. CASSEROLE)* heavy saucepan; combine sugar, milk, chocolate, syrup and salt. Cook, stirring constantly, over medium heat until sugar dissolves and mixture comes to a boil. *MICROWAVE AT HIGH 5 MINUTES, STIR.*

Cook to 234° (soft-ball stage), stirring only to prevent sticking. *TWICE* Remove from heat and add butter. *MICROWAVE AT HIGH.*

Cool without stirring to 110°. (After 10 minutes pan may be set in bowl of cool water, if desired.)

Add vanilla. Beat continuously with wooden spoon until fudge is thick and starts to lose its shine. Stir in nuts if desired.

Spread quickly in loaf pan. Cut while still slightly warm.

Converted Fudge

2 cups sugar
1 cup milk
2 squares unsweetened
   chocolate
1 tablespoon light corn syrup
⅛ teaspoon salt
2 tablespoons butter or
   margarine
1 teaspoon vanilla
½ cup chopped nuts, optional

Makes 1 pound

Butter a 9×5-in. or 10×6-in. loaf pan or dish; set aside. Butter a 3-qt. casserole. Combine sugar, milk, chocolate, syrup and salt in casserole. Cover. Microwave at High 5 minutes. Mix well to melt chocolate.

Microwave, uncovered, 10 to 14 minutes, stirring after 4 and 7 minutes, or until mixture reaches soft-ball stage (234°). Add butter.

Cool without stirring to 110°. (After 10 minutes pan may be set in bowl of cool water, if desired.) Add vanilla. Beat continuously with wooden spoon until fudge is thick and starts to lose its shine. Stir in nuts if desired. Spread quickly in loaf dish. Cut while still slightly warm.

12 to 24 minutes

Similar amount ingredients

Divinity

Microwaved divinity is stirred only once during cooking. Substitute a 3-qt. casserole for the 2-qt. saucepan to contain the high-boiling mixture. Use the cold water test to determine when syrup has reached the hard-ball stage.

Converted Divinity

2½ cups sugar
 ½ cup light corn syrup
 ½ cup water
 ⅛ teaspoon salt
 2 egg whites
 1 teaspoon vanilla
 ½ to 1 cup chopped nuts

Makes about 1¼ pounds

In 3-qt. casserole combine sugar, syrup, water and salt. Microwave at High 5 minutes. Stir well. Microwave 8 to 12 minutes, or until mixture reaches hard-ball stage. (260°.)

Immediately beat the egg whites until stiff peaks form. Slowly pour syrup over egg whites, beating at high speed with electric mixer.

Add vanilla. Continue beating 4 to 5 minutes, or until mixture holds its shape and starts to lose its gloss. Fold in chopped nuts.

Quickly drop heaping teaspoonfuls onto waxed paper or spread into a lightly buttered 10×6-in. dish and cut into pieces.

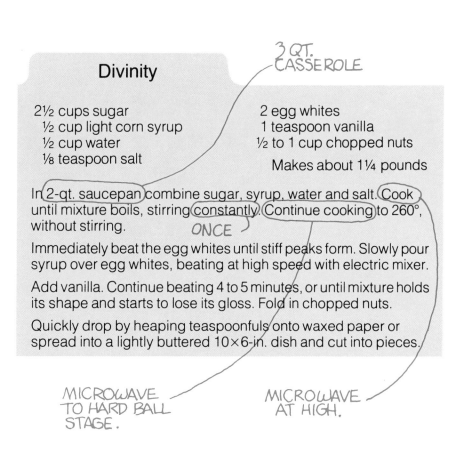

Divinity

3 QT. CASSEROLE

2½ cups sugar
 ½ cup light corn syrup
 ½ cup water
 ⅛ teaspoon salt

2 egg whites
1 teaspoon vanilla
½ to 1 cup chopped nuts

Makes about 1¼ pounds

In 2-qt. saucepan combine sugar, syrup, water and salt. Cook until mixture boils, stirring constantly. Continue cooking to 260°, without stirring. ONCE

Immediately beat the egg whites until stiff peaks form. Slowly pour syrup over egg whites, beating at high speed with electric mixer.

Add vanilla. Continue beating 4 to 5 minutes, or until mixture holds its shape and starts to lose its gloss. Fold in chopped nuts.

Quickly drop by heaping teaspoonfuls onto waxed paper or spread into a lightly buttered 10×6-in. dish and cut into pieces.

MICROWAVE TO HARD BALL STAGE.

MICROWAVE AT HIGH.

11 to 20 minutes

Similar amount ingredients

Adapting Jams & Jellies

Microwaving simplifies preparation of small batches of jam or jelly and keeps you and your kitchen cool. Make a little fresh jam or jelly as a treat for the family breakfast or a quick and easy gift for a friend.

Since microwaving exaggerates boiling of sugary liquids, it is important to make jams and jellies in small quantities, using a casserole which is large enough to contain boiling.

If you are a home gardener, pick fruits and berries as they ripen. The small batches are easy to microwave, and results will be more flavorful than a large batch of conventional jelly which includes overripe and underripe fruit.

For the sample, we selected a jelly recipe which calls for bottled fruit juice because it is available all year long. If you wish to make juice from fresh fruit, microwave the fruit without water until very soft, then strain juice through a jelly bag.

Small batches of jam and jelly can be stored in the refrigerator without sealing. If you wish to store them at room temperature, seal with paraffin. Melt the paraffin conventionally. Manufacturers recommend using a double boiler. Paraffin is transparent to microwave energy and will not melt in the microwave oven.

Do not attempt to can in the microwave oven. Canning requires prolonged high temperatures to kill bacteria, especially with vegetables which are low in acidity. In a microwave oven you cannot be certain that all the food has reached and maintained the temperature needed to preserve it.

Jelly is done when it coats a metal spoon or when two large drops on the edge of a spoon run together to form a single drop.

Converted Grape Jelly

Prepare 3 glasses & lids if desired.

> 1 cup bottled unsweetened
>   grape juice
> ½ cup water
> ½ pkg. (approximately 2 table-
>   spoons and 1 teaspoon -
>   ⅞-oz.) fruit pectin
> 1¾ cups sugar
>   Melted paraffin

>   Makes 2½ 8-oz. glasses

Combine grape juice, water and pectin in 2-qt. casserole. Microwave at High 4½ to 7½ minutes, or until mixture boils.

Stir in sugar. Microwave at 50% (Medium) 8 to 12 minutes, or until mixture thickens slightly and coats a metal spoon, stirring once during cooking to dissolve the sugar. Skim off foam.

If desired, ladle into glasses, wipe rims well and seal with paraffin. When glasses are cold, cover with lids. Jelly can also be stored in refrigerator. Paraffin is not needed.

7 to 15 minutes

1½ cups liquid

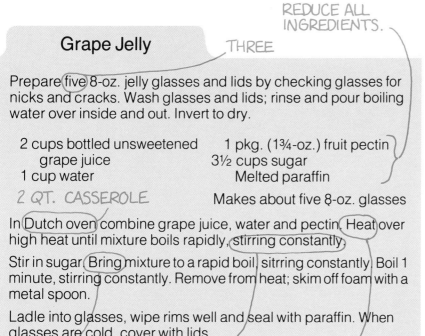

REDUCE ALL INGREDIENTS.

Grape Jelly

THREE

Prepare ~~five~~ 8-oz. jelly glasses and lids by checking glasses for nicks and cracks. Wash glasses and lids; rinse and pour boiling water over inside and out. Invert to dry.

2 cups bottled unsweetened grape juice	1 pkg. (1¾-oz.) fruit pectin
1 cup water	3½ cups sugar
	Melted paraffin

2 QT. CASSEROLE

Makes about five 8-oz. glasses

In ~~Dutch oven~~ combine grape juice, water and pectin. ~~Heat~~ over high heat until mixture boils rapidly, ~~stirring constantly~~.

Stir in sugar. ~~Bring~~ mixture to a rapid boil, ~~sitrring constantly~~. Boil 1 minute, stirring constantly. Remove from heat; skim off foam with a metal spoon.

Ladle into glasses, wipe rims well and seal with paraffin. When glasses are cold, cover with lids.

MICROWAVE AT 50% (MEDIUM).

OMIT

MICROWAVE AT HIGH

Index

In this index, recipe names printed in regular type are the conventional and microwave recipes used as samples in the book. Recipe names printed in italics refer to other popular dishes, which have not been used in the book, but can be converted by following the guidelines on the page indicated.

Recipes which do not convert well are also printed in italics and labeled "not suitable". When a page number occurs, it refers to an explanation in the text. Many recipes which are not suitable for conversion can be formulated for microwave and may be found in a microwave cookbook.